FRESH
BENTO

Affordable, Healthy Box Lunches Your Kids Will Adore

WENDY THORPE COPLEY

TUTTLE Publishing

Tokyo | Rutland, Vermont | Singapore

CONTENTS

Alphabet Bentos

Number Bentos

Color Bentos

WHY I WROTE THIS BOOK

When my boys were small, both their preschool and kindergartens classes focused on one letter, number or color per week. Their activities, art projects and lessons all revolved around these weekly themes and we also spent time at home talking about words that started with the letter of the week, as well as counting to the weekly number and identifying items around our home that were the color they were currently learning about. And as a bento-packing parent I, of course, made them lunches and snacks focusing on these themes—partly to reinforce their learning and partly to challenge myself and stretch my creativity.

When it came time for me to find a unifying idea for this book, the sequel to *Everyday Bento*, I thought back to those years and all the fun my kids and I had focusing on those lessons. The idea of creating a collection of bentos centered on those early lessons was born.

In this book, you'll find a bento box for every letter of the alphabet, for the numbers 1 to 10 and for a rainbow of colors. The letter bentos focus on foods and words that start with each letter—from alien avocados to zesty zucchini zeros. Kids can have fun looking at the bento boxes and identifying all the items that match the letter of the week. Some letters—like P and C—have so many foods that you could never fit them all into a single bento box. Others—X, I'm looking at you—have virtually no foods to match them so instead I focus on food art (in this case, x-ray sandwiches) and the letter itself. The number bento boxes highlight a few themes associated with that number—5-sided stars and 3-sided triangles, for example—and include foods in multiples of that number. And the color bentos are filled with foods and accessories that reflect the star of the show—a brown bagel bear, a pink shrimp or a juicy red apple. (I know you want

to know what's in the blue lunch. You'll see when you get to that chapter!)

I understand that not every bento in this book will work perfectly for every kid but they can all be adapted to work for your family. Be flexible when you are packing your bentos and use these instructions as a jumping-off point! I know some of the foods I use in this book might be challenging to some kids but they also might be a gentle nudge to try something new. I've included a list of foods and themes for each letter so if one of the bentos showcases a food that your child absolutely won't eat, you can select another from the list. And if rainbows are not your style, you can switch to robots, rhinos or roses. Some of the bentos will look really large or really small for your child. Consider what her appetite is like and adjust the portions up or down accordingly.

And finally, I know it can be frustrating to see me using lots of tools and accessories that you don't have. If you want to make creative bento boxes, I do recommend that you start with a few basic supplies—a set of silicone cups in several colors, some basic cookie cutters and a few decorative picks—but a huge collection of supplies really isn't necessary. It's definitely helpful to have a lot of special equipment and it can often speed up morning lunch packing considerably, but you can be really creative with a knife or scissors.

Finally, before you begin your bento journey I want to encourage you to involve your kids in the process. After the publication of *Everyday Bento*, I was surprised to learn how many children used it to start packing their own lunches. I shouldn't have been surprised by that, but I was! Some kids will pick up the book and dive right in on their own, but if yours are more reluctant you can encourage them to get involved in smaller ways. Ask them what their favorite foods are and pack a lunch revolving around that. Bring them to the store with you to shop for the week's food. Choose their favorite characters or activities and brainstorm ways they can be incorporated into a lunch. But mostly, just have fun with your child exploring new foods and a fun activity that you can spend time on together.

Happy bento-ing!

Wendy Thorpe Copley

Wendy Thorpe Copley

OPPOSITE PAGE, TOP TO BOTTOM Cheese letters, prosciutto twists and a B-themed bento box: what could be better? **TOP** There's no limit to the bento boxes you can create. A brown bear box centers on a color but also playfully pulls in letters too.

BENTO BOX BASICS

The Benefits of Making Bento Box Lunches

They're fun! Making decorative bentos is an enjoyable creative outlet. Both parents and kids can have fun planning and preparing fun lunches either by themselves or as a team. Mornings can be hectic and full of chores, but taking a few minutes to make a beautiful bento box starts the day off on a positive note.

They're economical. Packing lunches at home to bring to school saves money. You don't have to pay for school lunch and you also save money by reinventing leftovers from dinner, packing up the remaining berries from breakfast, or using the last few vegetables in the crisper.

They generate less waste. Pre-packaged lunches and school lunches generate a great deal of paper and plastic packaging waste, and traditional sack lunches with their plastic bags and single-serving snacks aren't much better. Packing food into a reusable box with reusable accessories generates no waste at all.

You have better control over ingredients. The only way to know exactly what food your child is eating is to prepare it yourself. With bento boxes you are free to choose organic fruits and vegetables, nitrite-free meats, and foods that are lower in sodium. You can also indulge in the occasional not-so-healthy treat if you like, but the choice is yours.

BASIC TECHNIQUES

Balance

An important goal when making a bento is to balance the types of foods in the box—proteins, produce, grains—and also to achieve a variety of flavors and textures. Shoot for packing at least five different colors into your bentos. This helps to ensure that you're getting lots of healthy fruits and veggies in your bento box.

Pack the Box Tightly

When you're packing a bento, it is important to fill the box completely. If the food isn't packed snugly and filled up to the top rim of the box, everything will mix together and the little bit of extra time you spent to make your meal attractive will have been wasted. When you pack a bento tightly, there's no extra space in the box and if there aren't any extra spaces, the food will stay in place when the box is tilted because it won't have anywhere to go. After you pack the main components, look for any extra spaces. If you find some, plug them up with smaller bites. Grapes, cubes of cheese, berries, and cherry tomatoes are wonderful for filling these little gaps. If you are using a box with a lot of dividers, this is less of a concern because the dividers will help keep things from moving around.

Pack the Box Neatly

One of the easiest ways to make a bento look attractive is simply to pack it neatly. Think about where each item will go before you put it in the box. When items are added, take a few seconds to decide on the best way to present them—crackers can be stacked, vegetable sticks lined up, and any marred pieces of fruit can be tucked under prettier ones.

Enjoy It!

Most importantly, have fun! Enjoy the beauty of colorful fruit and vegetables and think of creative ways to use your supplies. Add something that will make the person you're packing the lunch for smile, or if you're packing for yourself, put in a favorite treat to make your lunch extra special.

CHOOSING A BOX

Bento boxes come in a vast array of sizes, shapes, and materials. They range in price from just a few dollars for a small plastic box to well over $50 for a fancy stainless-steel model with all the bells and whistles with integrated thermal jars that keep part of the meal warm until lunchtime. With this many choices, it can be tough to know what bento box is right for you. Before you make a decision consider how much food you need to pack, the material that the box is made from, and the cost. Some people find it helpful to have multiple bento boxes to use throughout the week. This makes it easier to partially fill one lunch box the night before while another lunch box is in the dishwasher.

Stainless Steel Bento Boxes

Stainless steel lunch boxes are generally pricey, but they are very sturdy and will last for many years with minimal care. I've owned some of the metal lunch boxes you'll see in this book for more than eight years and they are still in great shape! They can take quite a bit of abuse without a lot of damage, but if your child is prone to losing his belongings you might want to use a less expensive box. Another issue with metal boxes is that they are usually not leak-proof and they can be heavy for young kids to carry.

Plastic Bento Boxes

Plastic bento boxes come in all shapes and sizes. Some of my favorites are ones that are divided into multiple sections with silicone seals that make them air-tight and leak-proof. I also like classic Japanese single-layer, single-compartment boxes and double-decker stacking boxes because they offer unlimited flexibility in how you can pack them. One of the best things about plastic bentos though is that they are usually very economical. This lower price allows you to buy multiple boxes so you can have the perfect container for the foods you want to pack on any given day.

Bento Boxes with Fun Shapes

If you ask my kids which of the bento boxes in my vast collection are their favorites, they'll probably name the boxes in fun shapes. You can find bento boxes that are shaped like animals, houses, cars, spheres and even hamburgers! While these lunch boxes are fun to use on occasion, I find their odd shapes can often be difficult to pack.

EQUIPMENT FOR MAKING CUTE BENTO BOXES

Having a variety of accessories on hand makes packing cute lunches nearly effortless, but not only that—they're really fun to collect! It's pretty easy to find tools that are made specifically for bento boxes online now—look for dedicated bento shops as well as checking big online retailers. You can also find a lot of fun stuff in the baking section of kitchen or department stores.

Alphabet Cutters

I use letter cutters from several different sets to make the lunches in this book but a single set should be plenty for most bento packers. Both metal or plastic cutters work well. Anything between 1–3 in. (2.5–7.5 cm) is a good size.

Number Cutters

Some alphabet cutter sets include numbers, but if they don't you will want to invest in a separate set of number cutters. I recommend something between 1–3 in. (2.5–7.5 cm) tall for the most versatility.

Shape Cutters

A variety of shape cutters makes it easy to create fun lunch boxes. Start with any cookie cutters you have on hand and add to your collection when you find something inspiring. Metal cutters are sturdy and cut through almost anything—including dense vegetables. Plastic cutters are more economical and they often come in variety packs based around holidays, seasons or other themes.

Stamping Cutters

Plunger or stamping cutters serve a dual purpose. The outside edge cuts a basic shape and the internal stamping plate adds decorative details. This kind of cutter works well on bread, cheese and melon slices.

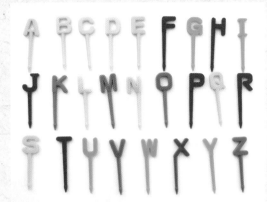

Alphabet Picks

Alphabet picks are an easy way to signify which letter your bento box is meant to represent. The sets I've come across usually have one of each letter so if you'd like to use them to spell words you might want to get 2 or 3 sets.

Decorative Picks

Decorative picks are cute and functional. Use them in place of a fork to pick up small items while you're eating your bento meal, or thread chunks of food on them for an appealing presentation. My favorite picks are the ones that are specifically designed to be used in bento boxes, because they are sturdy and can be reused over and over. Disposable cupcake picks made with wood and paper are inexpensive and easy to find in craft and grocery stores. You can even make your own decorative picks with toothpicks and stickers!

Silicone Cups

I use silicone cups in many of the bento boxes in this book because they are handy in many ways. Use them to separate foods from each other or to contain smaller items like berries or crackers. They are also a great way to add a pop of color for more visual appeal. While you can use paper or foil cups, I prefer silicone because they are flexible enough to fit any space, stand up to moisture and they are almost indestructible.

Knives and Scissors

Though cutters and picks are fun, all you really need to make beautiful bento lunches are a sharp knife and a pair of kitchen scissors. Use knives to slice fruits and vegetables, cube cheese, cut sandwiches into strips or triangles among other tasks. Kitchen scissors can perform many of the same tasks but they give you an extra level of control when you are making more artistic cuts. They are particularly helpful when cutting details from nori or fruit leather.

Lidded Containers

Leak-proof, lidded containers are helpful when you're packing liquid or semi-liquid foods. Small containers can be used for dips or dressings. Larger ones are great for yogurt or applesauce.

Food-Safe Marking Pens

I love these markers that use food coloring instead of regular ink for adding details to lunch box creations. They work best on bread, cheese, crackers and other dry, firm surfaces.

Rice (Onigiri) Molds

Rice or onigiri molds are available from retailers that sell Japanese kitchen goods. Use them to mold cooked rice into decorative shapes.

Punches

Use punches designed specifically for bento lunches to punch faces or other shapes out of nori seaweed. Regular paper punches designed for crafting can also be used for this purpose.

Cupcake Rings

Cupcake rings are primarily decorative but they add a nice touch to a lunch box.

PLANNING AHEAD

There's no denying it—packing an elaborate bento box on a weekday morning can be a challenge! Especially in the midst of all the chaos of breakfast, finding kids' shoes, and getting ready for work! But if you do a few of the tasks in advance everything goes much more smoothly and it can actually bring a little fun to the morning routine. Here are a few tips that will make it easier to pack cute lunches:

Write or Sketch your Plan for the Lunch in Advance

It's really hard to pull a creative bento box together on the spur of the moment—particularly if you are trying to stick with a specific theme. Making a written plan can help. Try sketching a rough drawing of the lunch you are planning and jot down a list of ingredients you'd like to use. This doesn't have to be super detailed or an artistic masterpiece—just a guide to help you organize your thoughts. It can also help show you what ingredients you need to buy or which equipment you should pull together.

Prep What You Can the Night Before

Prepping and packing for tomorrow's lunch the evening before makes a world of difference the next morning. Many foods can sit overnight in a bento box without suffering at all. Most whole fruits and vegetables do well, as do sandwiches, dips, yogurt, applesauce and rice. I've found that shapes cut from cheese, fruit leather, nori, fruit and vegetables tend to curl, dry up or get soggy so those are best prepared in the morning. Crackers, popcorn, rice cakes or any other crispy items should also be added at the last minute. Other items require that they be made in advance because there just aren't enough hours in the morning to prepare them. If you're baking something for a lunch, you can prepare it, let it cool and then add it to the lunch box in the morning.

Stock Your Freezer

It can be useful to have a stash of lunch items in your freezer for times when you can't prepare everything fresh. Packaging items up in single portion sizes allows you to grab just what you need and they also are easier to defrost. Some things that freeze well include rice, meatballs, sausages, prepared meat dishes, muffins, bagels, berries. You can also purchase pre-made items for lunches such as egg rolls, waffles, dumplings, and meatballs.

ALPHABET
BENTOS

A is for Astronaut

Start your bento alphabet off with a trip to space! An astronaut sandwich encounters an alien avocado when she lands on the moon. She also encounters apples, apricots and various forms of almonds.

Avocado
Lemon slice
Almonds
1 slice of whole wheat
  white sandwich bread
1 slice of whole wheat
  brown sandwich bread
Almond butter
Apricot jam
Fruit leather, any flavor
Dried apricots
Apple

EQUIPMENT
Divided bento box
  (PlanetBox Rover)
Gingerbread man cutter
Kitchen shears
Red food-safe marker
Small bowl (or a large,
  round cookie cutter)
Flag decorative pick
American flag cupcake
  decoration
Food carving tool
Fruit Fresh powder

Assembly

1 Slice the avocado in half and remove the pit. Rub a lemon slice over the top of one of the halves to prevent it from browning.

2 Scoop a ball of avocado from the other avocado half. You want the ball to be close to the same size as the crater left by the pit. I've found a melon baller, or a metal measuring spoon works well for this, but you can use a regular spoon too if you want.

3 Place the avocado ball into the first half of the avocado and then use a knife to trim off any excess. Your goal is to fill the hole left by the pit and make the top of the avocado smooth.

4 Add two almonds to the avocado half to look like alien eyes. Cut a slit below the eyes with the tip of a knife to look like the alien's mouth. Add the avocado half to the bento box.

As IN THIS BENTO
Avocado, Almonds, Alien, Almond butter, Apricot jam, Astronaut, Apricot, America, Apple.

OTHER IDEAS FOR A
Acai berry, Acorn squash, Animal crackers, Applesauce, Artichoke, Arugula, Asparagus, Airplane, Alligator, Ambulance, Anchor, Ant, Automobile, Autumn.

5 Use the gingerbread man cutter to create two astronaut shapes from the white bread slice.

6 Spread almond butter and apricot jam on one of the pieces of bread. Use kitchen shears to cut a small rectangle (meant to be the astronaut's visor) from the fruit leather and "glue" it to the second piece of bread with a little almond butter.

7 Use the food-safe marker to decorate the bread to look like an astronaut's suit. Stripes and a control panel look good, but you can get a little creative here if you want.

8 Use a small bowl to cut a thin arch from the slice of wheat bread.

9 Place it at the bottom of the largest section of the bento box for the astronaut to stand on. Add the astronaut sandwich and a flag pick to the lunch box.

10 Fill a third section of the lunch box with dried apricots. Add the American flag cupcake decoration.

11 Cut the apple into large chunks. Trim them to fit in the last section of the lunch box, then remove the largest chunk and carve the letter "A" into the skin with the carving tool. (If you don't have a carving tool, you can also do this with a knife.) Sprinkle the exposed flesh of the apple with Fruit Fresh powder (or use another anti-browning technique) and place it in the box.

Variation

If you don't have a slice of wheat bread, you can cut the astronaut's "moon" from the heel of a loaf of white bread. Swiss cheese also looks great because the holes resemble craters on the moon.

B is for BBQ Beef

This lunch pulls together several short-cut grocery items for a warm and filling lunch. Pull the biscuit apart at lunchtime and fill it with barbecued beef for a tasty sandwich.

½ lb (225 g) Brussels sprouts, trimmed and halved

2 tablespoons olive oil

Cooked bacon, cut into small pieces (optional, but delicious)

One 16 oz (525 g) package refrigerated biscuit dough

One 15 oz (500 g) package refrigerated pulled barbecued beef

Strawberries

Blackberries

Burger-shaped cookies

EQUIPMENT

Divided bento box with built-in thermal jar (OmieBox)

Medium "B"-shaped cutter

Small bunny cutter

Square silicone baking cup

Small round silicone baking cup

Decorative picks: bumble-bee, bird, ball and boat

Assembly

1 Preheat oven to 400°F (205°C).

2 Drizzle olive oil on a baking sheet. Toss Brussels sprouts in the oil and season with salt and pepper.

3 Roast brussels sprouts for about 20 minutes or until golden brown and tender, tossing half-way through. If you'd like, add a little bit of chopped bacon to the sprouts during the last 5 minutes of cooking. Cool the sprouts to room temperature by putting them in the refrigerator while you prepare the rest of the lunch.

4 Meanwhile separate the biscuit dough into individual rounds, then cut them into B shapes with the cutter. Place the biscuits on a baking sheet, then bake according to package directions. Cool to room temperature. (Biscuits can be made the night before to save time in the morning.)

5 Preheat the thermal container by filling it with boiling water. Heat the barbecued beef according to package directions.

6 Empty the water out of the thermal jar, then add the beef and place the container in the bento box.

7 Add a biscuit to the larger side compartment in the bento box. Place the silicone cup in the compartment's remaining space, then fill with the Brussels sprouts and bacon.

8 Cut one of the larger strawberries into thin slices. Cut the slices into bunny shapes with the small bunny cutter.

9 Cut a few more strawberries into quarters, then toss with some blackberries and add them to the remaining compartment in the bento box. Top with the bunny berries.

10 Add the small silicone cup to the berry compartment, and fill with a few of the burger cookies.

11 Add the decorative picks to the Brussels sprouts.

Bs IN THIS BENTO

Biscuit, Brussels sprouts, Bacon, Berries, Burgers, Barbecued beef, Bunny, Bee, Bird, Ball, Boat.

OTHER IDEAS FOR B

Baba ghanoush, Bagel, Baklava, Banana, Banana bread, Beans, Beets, Bison, Blood oranges, Blue cheese, Blueberries, Bocconcini, Bok choy, Bologna, Brazil nut, Bread, Broccoli, Brownie, Butternut squash, Baby, Ballet, Balloon,

Barn, Baseball, Basket, Basketball, Bat, Bear, Bell, Bike, Black, Blocks, Blue, Bone, Book, Bottle, Boy, Brown, Bubble, Bucket, Bug, Bulldozer, Bus, Butterfly, Button.

C is for Crab

I don't think there is an easier alphabet lunch to pack than one for the letter C! The list of foods that start with C is long and filled with kid-approved choices. If cherries and clementines aren't favorites, swap them for carrots and cucumbers. How about a little cheddar cheese? The options are nearly endless.

Crispy Curried Chick Peas (see recipe on facing page)
Crab Salad (see recipe on facing page)
2 mini croissants
Red bell pepper
Cherries
Clementine

EQUIPMENT
Divided Bento Box (EasyLunchboxes)
Small round cutters
Googly eye decorative picks
Small "C"-shaped cutter

Assembly

1 Prepare the Crispy Curried Chick Peas (facing page).

2 While the chick peas are baking, assemble the Crab Salad sandwiches. Make the Crab Salad (facing page).

3 Split the mini croissants horizontally and fill each one with Crab Salad.

4 Use the small circle cutter to cut four crescent shapes from the bell pepper. At the same time, cut two ½ in. (1 cm) slivers of pepper for the crabs' mouths.

5 Use the C cutter to cut a "C" too.

6 Add the crescent shapes to the tips of the sandwiches to represent claws and stick the googly eye picks into the top of the sandwiches. Use kitchen shears to cut small slits in the croissants just below the eyes and insert the slivers of pepper in them. (The slits will disappear if you don't add the peppers.) Place the sandwiches in the main compartment of the lunch box.

7 Once the chick peas are out of the oven, allow them to cool and add them to the smallest section of the lunch box. Top with the red pepper "C."

8 Peel and section the clementine and add it to the last section of the bento box, along with some cherries.

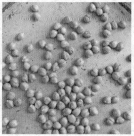

Crispy Curried Chick Peas

One 14.5 oz (400 g) can of chick peas, drained and rinsed
1 teaspoon olive oil
¾ teaspoon curry powder

1 Preheat oven to 425°F (220°C).

2 In a medium bowl, toss chick peas with olive oil until they are evenly coated. Sprinkle the curry powder over the chick peas and toss again until the spice is evenly distributed.

3 Spread chick peas over a baking sheet. Bake for about 25–30 minutes, or until chick peas are crispy and golden brown in spots

Crab Salad

If seafood isn't a favorite, swap roasted chicken for the crab in this salad.

¾ cup (100 g) cooked crab, picked over for shells (or use imitation crab)
2 tablespoons diced celery
2 tablespoons mayonnaise
½ teaspoon Old Bay seasoning

Combine all ingredients in a bowl and mix well.

Cs IN THIS BENTO
Crab, Celery, Chick peas, Curry, Clementines, Cherries.

OTHER IDEAS FOR C
Cabbage, Caesar salad, Cake, Candy, Cannellini beans, Cantaloupe, Carrots, Cashews, Cauliflower, Celery, Cereal, Cheddar cheese, Cheese, Cheesecake, Chestnut, Chia seeds, Chicken, Chips, Chives, Chocolate, Churros, Chutney, Cilantro, Cinnamon, Cocoa, Coconut, Coleslaw, Cookies, Corn, Corn tortilla, Cornbread, Corndog, Cottage cheese, Couscous, Crackers, Cranberries, Cream cheese, Crepe, Cucumber, Cupcake, Currants, Custard, Cactus, Cake, Camel, Camera, Camp, Candy, Cap, Car, Cassette tape, Castle, Cat, Caterpillar, Chameleon, Chef, Chick, Chimpanzee, Christmas, Circle, Circus, Clock, Cloud, Clover, Cookie, Cow, Crayon, Cream, Crown, Cube, Cup.

D is for Donut

Who doesn't love a donut? My kids would eat them every day if they could, but obviously they're not the healthiest choice for a lunch box treat. In this bento, I swap the deep-fried dough for a nutritious fake-out. I swap apple slices for pastry and sunflower seed butter for icing. The sprinkles get to stay!

Yellow bell pepper
½ recipe of Dilly Deviled
  Eggs (on page 27)
Green apple
Sunflower seed butter
  (or nut butter)
Sprinkles

EQUIPMENT
Divided bento box
  (EasyLunchboxes)
Duck-shaped cutter
Fruit Fresh powder
Small circle cutter
"D" decorative pick
Decorative waxed paper

Assembly

1 Place the deviled eggs into one of the small sections of the bento box.

2 Cut the bell pepper into large pieces, then use the cutter to cut a few duck shapes out. Chop the remaining pepper into strips or chunks, then add them to the bento box and top with the ducks. Insert a "D" pick into one of the ducks.

3 Slice the apple horizontally into ½ in. (1 cm) slices.

4 Sprinkle the slices with Fruit Fresh powder (or use another anti-browning technique).

5 Use a small circle cutter to remove the core from the center of the apple slices.

6 Spread sunflower seed butter on the apple slices. Do your best to leave a little border around the edge so the seed butter resembles the icing on a donut.

7 Scatter sprinkles on the seed butter, then add the apple "donuts" to the largest section of the bento box.

Tip

Bell pepper skins can be tough to cut through with a cookie cutter. If you're having a hard time breaking through the skin, press the cutter into the inner side of the pepper. You can also use a vegetable peeler to remove the skin from the pepper.

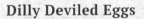

Dilly Deviled Eggs

2 hard-boiled eggs
1 tablespoon mayonnaise
½ teaspoon Dijon mustard
½ teaspoon white wine vinegar
¼ teaspoon chopped fresh dill
4 small dill sprigs

1 Cut the eggs in half and pop the yolks out into a small bowl.

2 Smash the yolks and combine with the remaining ingredients until smooth.

3 Divide the yolk mixture evenly between the four egg whites and top each egg with a sprig of dill.

Ds in this bento
Deviled egg, Dill, Donut, Duck.

Other ideas for D
Dahl, Daikon, Dark chocolate, Dashi, Dates, Dill pickle, Dim sum, Dip, Dolmas, Dragonfruit, Dried fruits, Drumsticks, Dumpling, Dad, Daisy, Deer, Dinosaur, Dog, Doll, Dolphin, Donkey, Dragon, Dragonfly, Dress, Dumptruck.

E is for Eggroll

This bento box is packed with Es: elephants, edamame, eclairs, emoji and the cutest eggroll ever! One could say it's an ECLECTIC mix! It's also EASY to pull together in the morning because it holds a lot of frozen staples.

Frozen egg rolls
Edamame (fresh or frozen)
1 slice Havarti or other white cheese
Fruit leather
Frozen mini eclairs

EQUIPMENT
Square bento box with removable dividers
Mini elephant-shaped cutter
Mini "E"-shaped cutter
½ in. (1.25 cm) circle cutter
Square silicone baking cup
Two decorative eye picks
Emoji cupcake decoration

Assembly

1 Remove divider from the bento box so you have one long and two small compartments.

2 Prepare the edamame and the eggroll according to package directions. Allow both to cool to room temperature.

3 Add a silicone baking cup to one of the smaller compartments and fill it with edamame.

4 Fold the slice of cheese in half, then use the mini elephant cutter to cut two shapes out of the cheese. Place the elephants on top of the edamame. Save the leftover cheese because you'll need it in a minute.

5 Use the mini "E" cutter to cut two shapes from the fruit leather. Place on top of the cheese elephants.

6 Add frozen eclairs to the other small compartment. You don't need to thaw them before packing—they will defrost by lunchtime. Top with the emoji cupcake decoration.

7 Fill the largest compartment with eggrolls. You should be able to fit two or three in the lunch box, depending on the size of your eggrolls.

8 Use the small circle cutter to cut a semicircle from the cheese. You can do this by positioning it half-way over one of the straight edges of the cheese. Insert the two eye picks in the eggroll on the top of the pile and then arrange the cheese semicircle underneath to make a face.

Es IN THIS BENTO

Edamame, Eclair, Eggroll, Elephant, Eyes, Emoji.

OTHER IDEAS FOR E

Eggnog, Eggplant, Egg, Elbow macaroni, Elderberry, Enchilada, Endive, English muffin, Earth, Earthquake, Eclipse, Envelope.

F is for Falafel

Build-your-own falafels are superfun at lunchtime. They might look complicated for a busy morning, but they actually come together very quickly. To save time in the morning, you can make the falafel the night before and pack the chilled patties in the lunch box in the morning. Or you can prepare the mixture the night before, shape and chill it overnight and give them a quick fry while you're preparing the rest of the lunch in the morning. I'll admit that fennel can be a tough sell for a lot of kids. To ease your child into the licorice flavor of this veggie, try pairing it with the sweet apple and the mild lemony dressing of this apple slaw.

1 mini pita pocket
4 Fabulous Fun Falafel patties (see recipe on facing page)
Tomato slices
Tzatziki sauce
Shredded lettuce
Crumbled feta cheese
Figs
Fennel and Apple Slaw (see recipe on facing page)
Fudge

EQUIPMENT
Divided bento box (Yumbox Panino)
3 rectangular silicone baking cups
Assorted decorative picks: "F," flamingo, frog, flower, and firetruck

Assembly

1 Cut the pita pocket in half and add it along one edge of the largest compartment of the bento box. Add the falafel patties on top.

2 Add the three silicone cups in the remaining space. Fill them with tomato slices, tzatziki sauce and shredded lettuce.

3 Trim and quarter a few figs. Add them to the lunch box and top them with a couple "F" picks.

4 Add a square of fudge to the smallest compartment in the bento box.

5 Fill the final section with the Fennel and Apple Slaw and top with the frog, flower, firetruck and flamingo picks.

Fs IN THIS BENTO
Falafel, Fennel, Feta, Figs, Fudge Firetruck, Flamingo, Flower, Frog.

OTHER IDEAS FOR F
Fajita, Fettuccine, Fish, Fish cake, Fish crackers, Fish sticks, Flapjacks, Flax seeds, Focaccia bread, Fortune cookie, Frankfurters, French fries, French toast, Fried rice, Frijoles, Fritters, Fruit salad, Fairy, Fall, Feet, Ferry, Fire, Firefighter, Fish, Flag, Flying saucer, Football, Fox.

Fabulous Fun Falafel (makes 14 patties)

One 14.5 oz (400 g) can of
  chickpeas, drained and
  rinsed
⅓ cup (20 g) fresh Italian
  parsley
⅓ cup (20 g) fresh cilantro
2 cloves garlic
1 tablespoon lemon juice
Zest of one lemon
½ teaspoon salt
½ teaspoon cumin
1 teaspoon baking powder
2–4 tablespoons flour
Olive oil, for frying

1 Combine all ingredients
except the flour in a food
processor and pulse until
everything is uniformly
chopped. Scrape down
the sides occasionally
so everything gets incor-
porated. You want the
mixture to be finely chopped,
but stop before it's a paste.

2 Add flour a tablespoon
at a time, stopping once the
mixture sticks together when
it's rolled in a ball.

3 Cover the mixture and
chill it in the refrigerator for
at least an hour to allow all
the flavors to blend.

4 Once the mixture has
chilled, divide it into balls
with a 2-tablespoon scoop.
Gently pat each ball into a
small patty with your hands.

5 Heat ¼ in. (5 mm) of
olive oil in a sauté pan
over medium heat until it
shimmers. Place half the
falafel patties in the pan
and cook for 2–3 minutes
on each side until a golden-
brown crust forms.

6 Remove falafel patties
from pan and drain on paper
towels to absorb excess oil.

7 Repeat steps 5–6 with
the remaining patties.

Fennel and Apple Slaw (2 servings)

2 teaspoons lemon juice
2 teaspoons extra virgin
  olive oil
½ teaspoon sugar
Salt and pepper
½ cup (60 g) fennel, cut
  into matchstick pieces
½ cup (60 g) apple, cut into
  matchstick pieces

1 Add lemon juice, olive
oil, sugar, salt and pepper
to a bowl and whisk until
combined.

2 Add in fennel and apple
and toss until fully coated
with the dressing.

G is for Gyoza

There are plenty of kid-friendly foods that start with G, so putting together a G lunch is fun and fast. I keep a stash of frozen gyoza in my freezer at all times because my kids love them and they reheat in the microwave in just a couple of minutes.

4 gyoza
Fruit leather
Granola bar
Grapes
Ruby red grapefruit
Steamed green beans

EQUIPMENT
Divided bento box (PlanetBox Rover)
Glasses and gem decorative picks
Green silicone leaf
"g"-shaped cutter

Assembly

1 Insert the glasses picks into the gyoza, positioning them about the curve so they look like smiling faces. Put the silicone leaf in the largest compartment of the bento box, then add the gyoza on top of it.

2 Cut a "g" shape out of the fruit leather with the "g" cutter. Peel the cut shape off the plastic backing, add the granola bar to the bento box and top with the fruit leather.

3 Cut a handful of grapes in half (this is so they'll lay flat in the lunch box), then cut a few thin wedges of grapefruit. Put a line of grapes in the bento box, then top with the grapefruit slices.

4 Trim the green beans to the length of the remaining compartment in the lunch box. Tuck a few gem picks into the beans.

Gs IN THIS BENTO

Gyoza, Glasses, Green, Granola, Grapes, Grapefruit, Green beans, Gems.

OTHER IDEAS FOR **G**

Garbanzo beans, Garlic,
Garlic bread, Gelatin, Ginger,
Ginger snaps, Gingerbread,
Gnocchi, Goat cheese,
Goji berry, Gooseberry,
Graham crackers, Green olives,
Green pepper, Guacamole, Guava,
Galaxy, Garden, Ghost,
Gingerbread man, Giraffe, Girl,
Goat, Goldfish, Gorilla, Grass,
Grasshopper, Guitar.

H is for House

I know the houses in this bento box look complicated to make, but trust me—they come together quickly with a few strategic cuts of a knife and some scraps of meat and cheese. Honeydew hearts and herb pita chips with hummus for dipping round out this happy H lunch.

2 slices sandwich bread (I used one slice of white and one slice of wheat to make the houses look different, but you can use two of the same if you only have one kind of bread on hand)
Deli ham
Havarti cheese
Mustard, mayo or other condiments
Snow peas
Honeydew melon
Hummus
Herb-flavored pita chips

EQUIPMENT
House-shaped, two-tier bento box
Black food-safe marker
Small, heart-shaped cutter
Small, rectangular silicone cup
Small "H" cutter
Decorative silicone food divider

Assembly

1 Assemble a sandwich using the bread, ham, Havarti and your preferred condiments.

2 Trim the crusts off the bread to make a rectangle. Do not discard the scraps! You'll use them in a minute.

3 Cut the sandwich into three rectangles of varying sizes. Trim the tops to turn them into houses.

4 Cut doors, windows and eaves from the scraps you cut off the edges of the sandwiches. I make doors from ham, windows from cheese and the eaves from the bread crusts. Attach the decorations by adding a little mayonnaise or mustard to the backs of the scraps as "glue" and pressing them onto the house shapes. Add further details with the food marker. Add the houses to one of the layers of the bento box.

5 Fill the space around the houses with the sugar snap peas, trimming the veggies to fit the space as necessary. The peas should be packed pretty tightly to prevent the sandwiches from moving around when the lunch is being transported.

6 Cut 1 or 2 slices of honeydew about ½ in (1 cm) thick. Use the cutter to cut several small hearts from the melon slice. Put them along the long edge of the second tier of the lunch box, with any imperfectly cut shapes hidden on the bottom row. Place the food divider up against the side of the melon.

7 Fill a small cup with hummus. Cut an "H" from the Havarti cheese and put in on top of the hummus. Place it in the lunch box and fill in the rest of the space with the pita chips.

Hs IN THIS BENTO

Ham, Herbs, Honeydew, Hummus, Heart, House.

OTHER IDEAS FOR H

Halibut, Haloumi, Hamburger, Hash browns, Hazelnut, Hazelnut spread, Hearts of palm, Hoagie, Hominy, Honey, Horseradish, Hot chocolate, Hot dog, Huckleberries, Halloween, Hammer, Hamster, Hand, Hat, Hedgehog, Hexagon.

I is for Ice Cream

Ice cream for lunch?? Have I gone crazy? Nope—this fake-out "ice cream" is made entirely from fruit and make kids *and* parents happy. Spin frozen bananas in the food processor along with raspberries or another kind of frozen fruit to make a healthy lunch-time treat. A few rainbow sprinkles add to the effect. Round out the rest of the lunch with ice-cream shaped sandwiches for grains and protein and an Italian salad for some veggies.

1 serving All-Fruit "Ice Cream"
  (see recipe on facing page)
Iceberg lettuce
Carrots
Italian dressing
Clementines
2 slices whole wheat bread
1 slice cheddar cheese
1 slice provolone cheese
Sandwich fillings and condiments

EQUIPMENT
Divided bento box with integrated
  thermal jar (OmieBox)
Rainbow sprinkles
Ice cream cone and popsicle cutters
Small screw-top jar
Decorative picks: "I" and insects

Assembly

1 Fill the thermal jar with the All-Fruit "Ice Cream" and put it in the freezer to keep it from melting while you prepare the rest of the lunch.

2 Chop the lettuce and slice a carrot. Place them in one of the compartments in the lunch box. Fill a small jar with Italian dressing and nestle it in the lunch box with the salad. Add a ladybug, bumblebee and "I" picks to the salad.

3 Peel and section two clementines and add spread them out in the bottom of the third section of the lunch box.

4 Cut two popsicle and two ice cream cone shapes from the bread. Press the dull side of a butter knife into one of the ice cream cone shapes in a crisscross pattern. Use the popsicle cutter to cut a shape from the cheddar cheese and the ice cream cone cutter to cut a shape from the provolone, positioning them so that you are only cutting the ice cream portions of the images. (see photo)

5 Assemble the sandwiches using the fillings of your choice. Place the sandwiches on top of the clementine wedges.

6 Place the thermal jar with the "ice cream" in the lunch box. Top it with a few sprinkles and then screw the lid on.

All-Fruit "Ice Cream"

2 extra-ripe bananas, sliced and frozen until firm
¼ cup (30 g) frozen raspberries

Combine bananas and raspberries in the bowl of a food processor and pulse until completely combined and pureed.

Tip

Place the thermal jar in the freezer while you prepare the all-fruit "ice cream." Chilling the bowl in advance helps keep the mixture frozen between morning prep and lunchtime.

Is IN THIS BENTO

Ice cream, Iceberg lettuce, Italian dressing, Insects.

OTHER IDEAS FOR I

Icing, Irish stew, Italian bread, Iceberg, Icicle, Iguana, Insect, Instrument, Iron, Island.

J is for Jellyfish

There aren't a lot of options for a J lunch. The list of foods that start with J is short but fortunately, a jellyfish sandwich swims into this lunch to save the day. You can showcase one of the J ingredients—jelly—by putting it on display in its own compartment and letting your child assemble her sandwich herself at lunchtime.

Jerky strips—beef, turkey or
   whatever your preference
Jicama
Chile-lime seasoning (such as
   Tajin brand)
Apricot fruit leather
2 slices white bread
Purple carrot
Jelly or jam—any flavor

EQUIPMENT
Divided bento box (Yumbox Panino)
Extra-large circle cutter
Kitchen shears
Small "J" cutter
1 in (2.5 cm) circle cutter
Crinkle cutter knife
Decorative picks: "J" and google eyes

Assembly

1 Place a few pieces of jerky into one of the smaller compartments in the bento box.

2 Cut a serving of jicama into rectangular chunks. Sprinkle with a little bit of chile-lime seasoning and place in the other small section of the lunch box.

3 Fill the smallest section of the bento box with jelly or jam. This can be spread on the bread from the "jellyfish" at lunchtime and is a fun way for your child to DIY their own sandwich. Add the "J" pick to the jelly. (Don't forget to include a small butter knife or spreader when you pack the lunch in a lunch bag so your child has a way to add the jelly to his sandwich!)

Js IN THIS BENTO
Jerky, Jicama, Jelly, Jellyfish

OTHER IDEAS FOR J
Jalapeño, Jam, Jambalaya,
Jell-O, Jelly beans, Juice,
Jack-o'-lantern, Jail, Japan,
Jewel, Jungle

4 Use the small "J" cutter to cut a few letters from the fruit leather. Place on top of the jicama.

5 Cut two pieces of bread with the circle cutter. Use the kitchen shears to cut a wavy border along the bottom edge of one of the bread circles. Place the cut circle on top of the second circle and use the edge as a guide to cut that piece too. Place the two bread slices one on top of the other in the large compartment of the bento box.

6 Cut a semi-circle by placing the small circle cutter partway on the fruit leather and pressing down. Add the semi-circle to the top of the bread, along with two google eye pics to make a face.

7 Use the crinkle cutter knife to slice the carrot into medium-long strips.

8 Place the carrot strips under and between the slices of bread to look like jellyfish tentacles.

K is for Kababs

Kababs (or really anything on a stick) are a fun way to eat food! I opted for kabocha squash and chicken here, but there are so many things that can be cubed and threaded onto a stick—tomatoes, cheese, bread, berries—the list goes on and on.

Soy-Roasted Squash (see recipe on facing page)
8 oz (225 g) package crescent roll dough
Roasted chicken, cubed
Kiwi
Kumquats

EQUIPMENT
Divided bento box (EasyLunchboxes)
Decorative skewers
Decorative picks: "K" and koala

Assembly

1 Prepare the Soy-Roasted Squash (see recipe on facing page).

2 Unroll the crescent roll dough but **do not** separate the pieces along the perforations. Gently close up any holes in the dough by pressing the separated edges together. Cut the dough into 1 in. (2.5 cm) strips.

3 Tie the strips into loose knots and place on a baking sheet. Cook according to package directions.

4 When knots are completely cool, place a few into one of the smaller compartments of the bento box. Poke the "K" pick into one of the knots.

5 Thread chunks of chicken and squash onto the skewers, alternating the meat and vegetables. Place the skewers into the largest section of the bento box.

6 Cut the kiwi in half using a decorative zigzag pattern. The easiest way to do this is the place the tip of a small, sharp knife into the kiwi, pushing it about halfway in. Pull the knife out, and reinsert it, angling it away from the first cut. Repeat these steps, going all the way around the circumference of the kiwi. When you've finished cutting, gently pull the two halves of the fruit apart.

7 Cut a few kumquats in half.

8 Place one of the kiwi halves in the remaining section of the bento box, then fill in any empty space with the kumquats. Insert the koala pick into the side of the kiwi.

> ### Tip
> Both the kabocha and the crescent knots can be prepared the night before to make lunch prep quicker in the morning!

Soy-Roasted Squash

1 lb (450 g) kabocha squash
1 tablespoon butter
2 teaspoons soy sauce

1 Preheat oven to 400ºF (205ºC).

2 Peel and seed the kabocha, then cut it into 1-in. (2.5-cm) cubes.

3 Melt butter and combine with soy sauce.

4 Pour butter mixture over kabocha and toss to coat. Spread squash in an even layer on a baking sheet.

5 Bake for 20 minutes or until squash is golden brown and easily pierced with a fork.

Tip Kumquats are one of the few citrus fruits that can be eaten whole. The skin and pith are sweet, with the pulp and juice are tart. If the batch of kumquats you have are too sour for your taste, cut them in half and squeeze out the juice and pulp. You'll be left with the sweet, citrusy peel and a delicious treat.

Ks IN THIS BENTO
Kabob, Kabocha, Kiwi, Kumquat, Knot, Koala.

OTHER IDEAS FOR K
Kale, Ketchup, Kidney beans, Kielbasa, Kiwi berries, Knish, Kohlrabi, Kangaroo, Kettle, Key, King, Kiss, Kite Kitty, Knee, Knife.

L is for Lettuce

Lettuce is an obvious choice to represent the letter L, so a simple salad covered with more Ls takes center stage in this lunch. Ham and cheese "lollipops" add a little extra fun and some light and fluffy ladyfingers complete the meal.

Lettuce
Red, orange and yellow bell pepper
1 slice sandwich bread
Butter
Garlic salt
Lemon Vinaigrette (see recipe on facing page)
2 slices deli ham
1 slice white American cheese
Ladyfingers

EQUIPMENT
Divided bento box (EasyLunchboxes)
"L" stamping cookie cutter
Small "L"-shaped cutter
Small bottle
Decorative heart picks

Assembly

1 Place a bed of lettuce in the largest compartment of the bento box.

2 Use the larger cutter to cut a rectangle from the slice of bread. Stamp the L into the bread using the other side of the cutter. Spread a thin layer of butter over the raised portions of the bread and sprinkle it lightly with garlic salt. Toast in a toaster oven until lightly browned. Add the crouton to the center of the lettuce.

3 Cut a chunk from each of the bell peppers. Use a vegetable peeler to remove some of the tough skin from each of the peppers. (This will make it easier to cut through the pepper with a plastic cookie cutter.) Use the small L cutter to cut 4–5 Ls from each color of pepper. Sprinkle the pepper Ls over the top of the salad.

4 Fill the small bottle with the Lemon Vinaigrette. Add it to the salad compartment.

5 Lay the two slices of ham on the cutting board, over-lapping them a little. Place the slice of cheese on top.

6 Trim the edges of the ham with no cheese covering it. Cut the ham and cheese lengthwise into 1 in. (2.5 cm) strips. Carefully roll the strips up to create a spiral pattern. Spear the spirals with the heart picks, pushing them all the way through so part of the stick comes out the bottom, resembling a lollipop. Add the "lollipops" to one of other sections of the lunch box.

7 Place a few ladyfingers in the remaining empty section of the bento box.

Lemon Vinaigrette

1 tablespoon lemon juice
1 tablespoon Olive oil
Pinch of salt
Pinch of ground black pepper

Combine all ingredients in a small bowl. Whisk until combined.

Ls IN THIS BENTO

Lemon, Lettuce, Ladyfinger, Lollipop, Love.

OTHER IDEAS FOR L

Lamb, Lasagna, Lemongrass, Lentils, Licorice, Lima beans, Lime, Linguine, Liverwurst, Lobster, Loquats, Lychees, Ladybug, Lamb, Leaf, Lego, Lightbulb, Lion, Lip, Lizard, Lock, Lunch.

M is for Meatballs

The meatball monsters in this lunch are so easy to make, but they add a lot of personality to any lunch box. IF you practice a little, it's easy to make the mouths smile or frown. You can also add a cute hat pick to the tops in addition to the eye picks. And if you don't have the eye picks, you can make eyes with a small circle of cheese and a dot of a food coloring.

Meatballs (frozen meatballs
  are a convenient option)
Small mozzarella balls (concigli)
Mouse-shaped crackers (Goldfish brand)
Mini muffin
Mango
Mini marshmallows

EQUIPMENT
Divided bento box (Yumbox original)
Decorative picks: googly eyes and "M"
Round silicone baking cup (optional)
Small melon baller

Assembly

1 If you're working with frozen meatballs, thaw them according to package directions and, if necessary, let them cool enough that you can easily work with them.

2 Cut a long, thin wedge shape out of each meatball to resemble a mouth. Add a googly eye pick to each meatball to make it look like a monster. Add the meatballs to the bento box.

3 Place a few mozzarella balls in a different section of the box and spear a couple with the M picks.

4 Add the mouse crackers to one compartment of the lunch box.

5 Place a silicone muffin cup in another section and put the mini muffin inside it. (The silicone cup isn't strictly necessary, but it will keep the muffin from getting banged around during transport—plus it looks nice!)

6 Cut two large slabs from either side of the mango pit. Use a small melon baller to scoop out spheres of mango and add them to the final large compartment in the bento box.

7 Finally, add a few mini marshmallows to the smallest compartment of the bento box.

> *Tip* If you don't have a melon ball tool, small metal measuring spoons work well to make the mango balls.

Ms IN THIS BENTO

Mango, Marshmallows, Meatballs, Mozzarella, Muffin, Monster, Mini, Mouse.

OTHER IDEAS FOR M

Maple, Mashed potatoes, Matcha, Mayonnaise, Meat, Meatloaf, Melon, Mesclun, Millet, Mint, Mousse, Muesli, Mulberries, Mushroom, Mustard, Magnet, Mail, Mermaid, Minecraft, Mitten, Mom, Money, Monkey, Moon, Motorcycle.

N is for Nutty Noodle Nest

The nest of nutty noodles in this meal makes for a hearty lunchtime entrée. The vegetables used can be swapped out according to taste or what you have on hand. It's a great recipe for using up small bits of leftovers from dinner the night before.

1 package ramen noodles
Round, wax-wrapped cheese (such as Babybel brand)
Assorted nuts
Red bell pepper
Carrot
Nutty Noodle Peanut Sauce (see recipe on facing page)
Hard-boiled egg
Nectarine
Nori

EQUIPMENT
Divided bento box (Yumbox Panino)
Black food coloring marker
Decorative picks: sword and "N"

Assembly

1 Cook ramen noodles according to package directions, but omitting seasoning packet. Drain noodles, then set aside to cool while you prepare the rest of the lunch.

2 Peel back the paper handle under the wax on one side of the piece of cheese. Snip off the wax piece with a pair of scissors then remove the paper backing. Fold the wax strip so that it forms a "V" shape. Press the point of the V into the wax on the back side of the cheese. Flip the cheese over and draw two eyes on the exposed bit of cheese using a black food coloring marker.

3 Put a handful of nuts into one of the sections of the bento box. Place the cheese ninja on top and poke a sword pick into it.

4 Slice the nectarine. Place in another section of the lunch box and insert an "N" pick in one of the slices.

Variations

If your child isn't a fan of red pepper or carrot, swap in an equal amount of another vegetable. Broccoli, sugar snap peas, or edamame will all work in this dish.

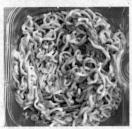

Nutty Noodle Peanut Sauce

1 tablespoon soy sauce
2 tablespoons peanut butter
¼ teaspoon sesame oil
¼ teaspoon honey
2 tablespoons hot water

Combine all ingredients in a bowl until fully combined. Toss with ramen noodles or use as a dipping sauce.

5 Finish preparing the noodles: Cut a chunk from the red bell pepper and thinly slice it so that you have about ¼ cup of strips. Peel the carrot, then use the peeler to shave off about ¼ cup of ribbons. Combine the noodles, the vegetables and the Nutty Noodle Peanut Sauce.

6 Place the noodles in the largest compartment of the lunch box and arrange into a nest shape. Cut the hard-boiled egg in half and place the two pieces in the center of the nest.

7 Cut the nori into squares and place them in the smallest section of the lunch box.

Ns IN THIS BENTO
Nectarines, Noodles, Nori, Nuts, Nest, Ninja.

OTHER IDEAS FOR N
Naan bread, Nachos, Nuggets, Nail, Name, Narwhal, Net, Newspaper, Nose, Note, Numbers.

O is for Owl and Octopus Onigiri

Onigiri—salted rice balls—are a staple of Japanese cuisine and a near perfect lunch box food. They are fast to make, delicious and they keep beautifully until lunchtime. I've made the simplest version for this lunch box—just rice with a little salt and nori for flavor and decoration—but you can fill them with leftover bits of meat, veggies or whatever else you have hanging around in your refrigerator.

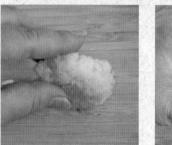

Sushi rice
Nori
Orange
Mini oatmeal cookies
Fruit leather

EQUIPMENT
Four-compartment bento box
Scissors
Medium and small circle cutters
Orange silicone baking cup
Decorative picks—"O" and octopus

Assembly

1 Prepare 2 cups of sushi rice according to the directions on the package.

2 Once the rice is cool enough to handle, shape the onigiri. Wet your hands and rub a healthy pinch of kosher salt between your palms. (Wetting your hands keeps the rice from sticking to them.) Pick up enough rice to comfortably fit in the palm of your hand and press it into a ball. To make a round onigiri, pat the rice into a disk shape. The edges of the disk will be a bit thinner at this point, so pat them back into an even thickness with your fingers. You can also roll the disk across the cutting board to firm up the edges. Repeat to make a second round onigiri.

3 To make a triangular onigiri: Wet and salt your hands, then form the rice into a ball and pat it into a disk shape. Form the triangle shape by pressing the

Tip Sometimes fruit leather shapes—particularly more intricate ones—tear when you try to peel them off the plastic backing. To avoid this, peel the leather up from the plastic before cutting it, then lay it loosely back down on the plastic. It should come up easily after cutting.

disc into the angle between you thumb and forefinger (see photo) then rotating it until you have three slightly rounded corners. Repeat to make a second triangular onigiri.

4 Cut two triangles of nori about the same size as the onigiri. Use a pair of sharp scissors to round one of the corners to look like the head of an octopus, then cut the bottom of the triangle to look like eight tentacles. Repeat with another piece of nori and then press the octopuses onto the top of each one of the triangular onigiri. Cut scraps of nori to look like the ears, eyes, beak and wings of an owl and then apply them to the round onigiri as shown. If you are having trouble getting the nori to stick to the rice, you can wet your finger slightly and rub it on the rice. The nori will adhere easily.

5 Place the onigiri into opposite corners of the bento box, stacking them on top of each other.

6 Cut an orange into wedges. Place them in the box and add the "O" and octopus picks.

7 Add the silicone cup to the remaining compartment, then fill it with the oatmeal cookies. Cut an O from the fruit leather using the two circle cutters then add it on top of the cookies.

Os IN THIS BENTO
Onigiri, Orange, Oatmeal cookies, Owl, Octopus.

OTHER IDEAS FOR O
Oatmeal, Oats, Okra, Olive oil, Olives, Omelet, Onion, Orzo, Ocean, Octagon, Orange, Ostrich, Otter.

P is for Pepperoni Pita Pizza

It can be difficult to know where to begin when you're packing a P lunch because there are so many foods that start with the letter. I solved this problem by picking every kid's favorite main course—pizza! Pita pizzas are quick to put together in the morning and kids love them. Round out this lunch with a selection of crunchy snacks, sweet fruit and kid-approved veggies.

Mini pita pockets
Pizza sauce (marinara works too)
Mozzarella cheese
Pepperoni
Peanut-butter-stuffed pretzels
Popcorn
Papaya
Red bell pepper
Peas
Pistachios

EQUIPMENT
Divided bento box (PlanetBox Rover)
Kitchen shears
Purple triangle silicone baking cup
Rectangle silicone baking cup
Decorative picks: "P," pineapple,
   panda, penguin
Small penguin cutter

Assembly

1 Make the pizzas: Place two of the mini pitas on a baking tray and spread on an even layer of pizza sauce. Top each pizza with a hearty sprinkle of mozzarella cheese.

2 To make the pepperoni Ps, cut a four pepperoni slices in half to make eight semi-circles. Cut smaller semi-circles from the inside of four of the semi-circles. Cut the remaining semi-circles into strips. Use the cut pieces of pepperoni to create Ps on top of the pizzas. Sprinkle any scraps around the edges.

3 Bake the pizzas at 375°F (190°C) in a toaster oven for 6 minutes or until the cheese is bubbly and browned in places. Cool the pizzas to room temperature and then stack them in the largest section of the bento box.

Assemble the rest of the lunch:

1 Add the peanut butter pretzels to the purple cup and place it on one side of one of the lunch box compartments. Fill the other side of the compartment with popcorn.

2 Prepare the papaya and cut a few slices. Place them in another section of the lunch box and add the P, panda, pineapple and penguin picks.

3 Cut a chunk from the red pepper and use the cutter to create a few penguin shapes. Chop the remaining piece of pepper into bite-sized pieces and add them to half of the remaining section of the lunch box. Top with the penguin shapes.

4 Add the rectangular silicone cup to the remaining empty space and fill it with the peas.

5 Finally, add a few pistachios to the small snack compartment.

Ps IN THIS BENTO

Papaya, Peanut butter, Pretzels, Peas, Pepperoni, Peppers, Pistachios, Pita bread, Pizza, Popcorn, Penguin, Panda, Pineapple.

OTHER IDEAS FOR P

Paella, Pancake, Pancetta, Parmesan cheese, Parsley, Parsnip, Passionfruit, Pasta, Peach, Pear, Pecans, Pepitas, Perogies, Persimmon, Pesto, Pickles, Pie, Pinto beans, Plantain, Plum, Polenta, Pomegranate, Poppy seed, Pork, Potato, Potstickers, Provolone, Prunes, Pudding, Pail, Paint, Paint box, Paint brush, Parrot, Paw, Peacock, Pen, Pencil, Phone, Pig, Pink, Pinwheel, Plane, Planet, Plant, Platypus,

Pocket, Polar bear, Police, Polka dots, Pony, Poop (emoji), Porcupine, Prince, Princess, Puffer fish, Pumpkin, Puppy, Purple.

Q is for Quesadilla

There aren't many foods that begin with Q and even fewer Q foods that most young kids know and like. Starting with a quesadilla as a major component of this lunch is a good start since this is a popular lunch item with lots of children. Try stretching your child's palate a little by including some options she may not be as familiar with: fresh quince is delicious if you can find it but quince jam might be a bit easier to locate. Quinoa is also pretty common in grocery stores. Mix it with veggies and a simple vinaigrette for a tasty grain salad, then top it with a queen's crown and some question marks to add more Qs to this lunch. A bell pepper quilt finishes the theme off nicely.

Yellow and red bell pepper (or other colored
  bell peppers of your choice)
Quinoa Salad (see recipe on facing page)
Quince jam
Quinoa crackers
Large flour tortilla
Grated cheddar or jack cheese

EQUIPMENT
Divided bento box (PlanetBox Rover)
Medium rectangle cutter
Crown-shaped cutter
Small question-mark-shaped cutter
Medium "Q"-shaped cutter
Small rectangular silicone baking cup

Assembly

1 Cut a chunk from each of the bell peppers and position them side by side on the cutting board. Place the rectangle cutter over both pieces of pepper and cut them so that one piece of pepper is just a little larger than the other. (You can also do this step with a knife, but the cutter ensures a clean, rectangle shape.)

2 Cut the smaller pepper piece into six equal squares and cut the larger piece into nine equal squares.

3 Arrange the pepper squares in a checkerboard pattern in one of the compartments of the bento box so that they look like a quilt.

4 Place the Quinoa Salad in another section of the lunch box. Cut a crown shape from another chunk of the yellow pepper and put it on top of the salad. Cut a few question marks from the remaining pepper scraps and add them on top of the salad too.

> ## Variations
> You can substitute almost any flat vegetable for the peppers when making the "quilt." Try cutting quarter inch planks of carrots or jicama into squares. Two colors of melon would also work well here.

Quinoa Salad

½ cup (50 g) prepared quinoa
1 tablespoon diced red bell pepper
1 tablespoon diced yellow bell pepper
2 tablespoons chopped, cooked broccoli
2 tablespoons balsamic vinaigrette

Place all ingredients in a bowl and stir to combine.

5 Fill a small container with some of the quince jam. Add it to the bento box with a stack of quinoa crackers.

6 Heat a skillet over medium heat. Make the quesadilla by sprinkling cheese across one of the tortillas, topping with the other and heating it in the skillet until the cheese is melted and the tortilla is brown in spots. Flip the quesadilla and toast the other side until it also is browned in spots.

7 Remove the quesadilla from the pan and cool for 2–3 minutes on a cutting board. Cut as many Q shapes with the cutter as you can. Add them to the largest section of the bento box.

Qs IN THIS BENTO
Quesadilla, Quince,
Quinoa, Queen,
Question, Quilt

OTHER IDEAS FOR **Q**
Quiche, Quarter,
Quasar,
Quill, Quiz

R is for Rainbow

Ravioli! Raspberries! Raisins! Rice cakes! There are plenty of delicious foods that start with the letter R and a healthy handful of R themes to go with them. I chose to make a rainbow the focal point of this bento box because nothing is more appealing at lunchtime than a tray filled with brightly colored vegetables.

Ravioli, any flavor
Grape or cherry tomatoes
Ranch dressing
Raisins
Raspberries
Romaine lettuce leaf
Rice cake
Ricotta cheese
Red, orange, yellow and green
  bell peppers

EQUIPMENT
Divided bento box
  (PlanetBox Rover)
4 nesting circle cutters—
  2.5 in. (6.5 cm), 2 in. (5 cm),
  1.5 in. (3.75 cm) and
  1 in. (2.5 cm)
Small sauce container
Assorted decorative picks:
  rings, rocket, rabbit,
  raccoon and the letter "R"

Assembly

1 Cook ravioli according to package directions. Cool and add a few to one of the sections of the bento box. (Save the remaining ravioli for another meal.)

2 Fill the sauce container with ranch dressing.

3 Spear a few tomatoes with the ring picks and add them to the bento box along with more tomatoes and the ranch dressing.

4 Poke the rest of the decorative picks into some raspberries and add to a third section of the bento box.

5 Line the largest compartment of the bento box with a romaine lettuce leaf.

6 Create a rainbow from the peppers. Cut semi-circles from each of the peppers. Use the largest circle cutter on the red pepper, the next largest on the orange and so on until you've cut the green pepper with the smallest cutter.

7 Turn the red, orange and yellow semi-circles into arcs by cutting them with the next smaller size of circle cutter. Use the 2 in. (5 cm) cutter on the 2.5 in. (6.5 cm) semi-circle of red pepper, the 1.5 in. (3.75 cm) cutter on the 2 in. (5 cm) semi-circle of orange pepper and so on.

8 Nest the arcs against each other, then trim the bottom so it's tidy.

9 Spread ricotta cheese on the rice cake, top with the pepper rainbow and place it on top of the romaine lettuce leaf.

10 Add raisins to the small treat compartment.

Tip If lunchtime is many hours away from the time this meal is packed, the rice cake might lose some of its crispiness. Avoid this problem by packing the ricotta cheese in a small containing and having your child spread it on the rice cake when it's time to eat.

Rs IN THIS BENTO

Raisins, Ranch dressing, Raspberries, Ravioli, Red pepper, Rice cake, Ricotta, Romaine lettuce, Rabbit, Raccoon, Rainbow, Ring, Rocket.

OTHER IDEAS FOR R

Racecar, Rain, Read, Red, Reindeer, Rhinoceros, Robot, Rock, Rock and Roll, Rooster, Rose, Radicchio, Radish, Ramen, Refried beans, Relish, Rueben, Rhubarb, Ribs, Rice, Rice crackers, Rice noodles, Rice pudding, Ritz crackers, Rolls, Roll-ups, Rye.

S is for Salmon and Spinach Sushi

Sushi is an obvious choice for an S-themed bento box! Of course, you can buy pre-made sushi rolls to lower the time it takes to pack lunch, but homemade sushi is fun to make and it's not as hard as you might think. Plus, you can add more ingredients that start with S when you make it yourself! I filled these rolls with spinach and smoked salmon and sprinkled sesame seeds on top. This lunch also features a strawberry snake and some snow peas.

Sushi rice
Nori seaweed sheets
Spinach
Smoked salmon
Sesame seeds
Snow peas
4 strawberries

EQUIPMENT
Single-tier bento box
Bamboo sushi rolling mat
Two pieces of baran
 (food dividers)
Mini fork
Icing googly eyes
Large "S"-shaped cutter
Decorative picks: seal
 and squirrel

Assembly

1 Place a piece of nori seaweed on a sushi rolling mat. Spread a thin, even layer of rice over the nori, leaving a 1 in. (2.5 cm) strip free along one edge. Place salmon and spinach in even layers across the rice.

2 Use the edge of the sushi rolling mat to double the rice over onto itself. Tuck the edge in to start forming a cylindrical shape then continue tightly rolling the sushi until you're near the end. Wet the edge of the nori that is free of rice with a little bit of water and then roll the sushi closed. The water should help the nori stick to itself.

3 Cut the sushi roll in half horizontally using a serrated knife. Cut the two halves into three equal pieces each for a total of six sushi rolls. Stand the rolls on end and

Ss IN THIS BENTO

Sesame seeds, Smoked Salmon, Snow peas, Spinach, Strawberries, Sushi, Snake, Seal, Squirrel.

OTHER IDEAS FOR S

Scones, Shish kabob, Shortbread, Shrimp, Smoothie, S'mores, Soba noodles, Soup, Spaghetti, Spring onions, Squash, Squid, Star fruit, Steak, String beans, String cheese, Sunflower seeds, Sweet potato, Swiss chard, Swiss cheese, Sailor, Santa, Scarecrow, School, Sea, Seahorse, Seal, Shamrock, Shark, Sheep, Ship, Shoe, Skate, Skateboard, Skeleton, Smile, Snail, Snowflake, Snowman, Soccer, Space, Spaceship, Spider, Square, Stamps, Star, Starfish, Stocking, Stop sign, Stripes, Sun, Sunglasses, Swan, Swimming, Swing, Sword.

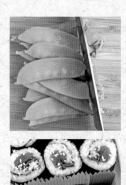    

sprinkle with sesame seeds. Place the sushi rolls in the middle of the bento box.

4 Trim the ends off the snow peas and pull off the tough fibers along the edges of the peas. Put them in one of the empty spaces in the bento box. Add the seal and squirrel decorative picks.

5 Cut one of the strawberries in one half and two quarters from top to bottom. Cut another strawberry into quarters. You'll use these pieces to make your snake. Slice the two remaining strawberries into thin slices.

6 Add two of the baran (food dividers) to the box next to the sushi to separate it from the strawberries. Put the thin-sliced strawberries in an even layer in the bento box. Layer some spinach leaves on top of the strawberries.

7 Arrange the half strawberry on top of the small bento fork with the tines of the fork sticking out to look like a forked tongue. Stick the icing eyes to the berry and place them on top of the spinach in the bento box. Arrange the rest of the quartered berries behind the snake's "head" to look like the body of the snake.

8 Place the S-shaped cutter on top of a piece of nori and cut around it with a knife or a pair of kitchen scissors. (If you can cut through the nori with just the cutter, that's great but I found it too difficult to manage.) Place the S cut out on top of the sushi.

Tip Spread sushi rice on a plate or tray and pop it in the refrigerator for a few minutes to cool it quickly if you are in a rush.

T is for Tofu

Tofu isn't a staple food in every American household, so it can be challenging for some kids. I've found that marinated, baked tofu is a great way to introduce this protein-rich food to children who might be reluctant to try it because the firm texture and sweet, tangy marinade are more appealing than softer, plain tofu.

Baked teriyaki tofu
Broccoli, lightly steamed
Cherry tomatoes
Tangerine
Tamari almonds
Tapioca
Chocolate sprinkles

EQUIPMENT
Divided bento box (Bentgo Kids)
Small tree cutter
Small smiley face cutter
Decorative picks: tree trunks, teddy bears, taxi, turtle, "T," and teddy bear in a tea cup
Small "T"-shaped cutter
Tweezers

Assembly

1 Stand a brick of baked tofu on one of its narrow sides and cut a ¼ in. (5 mm) slab off the broadest side. Use the tree cutter to cut a shape out of the cut piece of tofu. Remove the tree shape from the rectangle, then flip it over so the darker side shows and put it back into the hole. Insert the smiley face cutter a few millimeters into the tree, but don't cut all the way through it. A smiley outline should be cut into the tofu. Use the tip of a sharp paring knife to remove the eyes and mouth cut into the tree. Cut the remaining, thicker piece of tofu into strips. Add them to the bento box, then top with the tree decoration.

2 Insert the tree trunk picks into the stem end of a few of the broccoli pieces. Fill the remaining space in the tofu compartment with plain broccoli, then top with the pieces on the picks.

Ts IN THIS BENTO

Tofu, Tapioca, Tomatoes, Tangerine, Tamari almonds, Tree, Teddy bear, Tea cup, Taxi, Turtle.

OTHER IDEAS FOR T

Tarts, Tempeh, Tempura, Teriyaki, Toast, Tobiko, Tonkatsu, Tortellini, Tortilla chips, Tortillas, Trout, Truffle, Tuna, Turkey, Turnip, Tea pot, Telephone, Tennis, Tent, Thumb, Tiger, Tongue, Tooth, Toys, Tractor, Train, Triangle, Tricycle, Trolley, Truck, Tugboat, Tulip, Turkey.

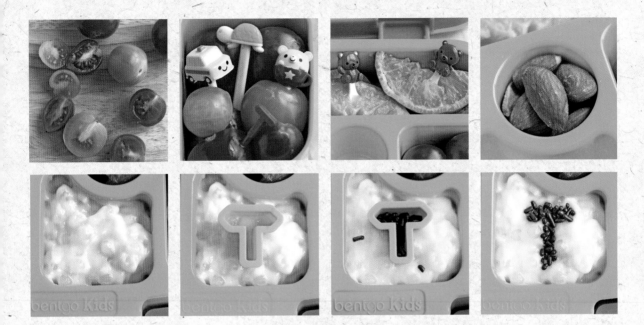

3 Cut the cherry tomatoes in half and add to one of the smaller compartments in the bento box. Spear some of the tomatoes with the taxi, turtle, tea cup and "T" decorative picks.

4 Cut some slices from the tangerine and add to another compartment. Add a few teddy bear picks.

5 Place some of the tamari almonds in the smallest compartment.

6 Spoon some tapioca pudding into the last compartment and put the small "T" cutter on top. Carefully pour some of the chocolate sprinkles into the cutter. Use the tweezers to spread the sprinkles into an even layer and gently press them into the pudding. Remove the cutter, leaving a chocolate "T" behind.

U is for Udon Noodles

Udon noodles, unicorns and underpants! A perfect lunch box for young kids. Chewy udon noodles are paired with a sweet honey sesame sauce and served cold for this lunch. I added tenkasu—crunchy tempura batter bits—to sprinkle on right before eating for a bit of extra texture. If you can't find these, you can use fried wonton strips or just skip them altogether. For the side dishes I added fruit with unicorn picks and cucumber cut to look like a pair of underpants. So silly and fun!

Honey-Sesame Udon Noodles (see recipe below)
Blackberries
Cucumber
Tenkasu (crunchy tempura batter bits)

EQUIPMENT
Divided bento box (Yumbox Panino)
Decorative picks: Unicorns and "U"

Assembly

1 Add the Honey-Sesame Udon Noodles to the main compartment of the lunch box. Sprinkle the sesame seeds on top.

2 Put some blackberries in one of the side compartments, then add some unicorn picks.

3 Cut a round slice of cucumber. Use a knife to cut it into an underpants shape, as shown. Peel and cut the rest of the cucumber into sticks. Add them to the bento box, then top with the underpants cut-out. Add the U decorative picks to the cucumbers.

4 Fill the snack compartment with the tenkasu.

Honey-Sesame Udon Noodles

7 oz (200 g) package udon noodles
1 teaspoon chopped garlic
1 tablespoon soy sauce
1 teaspoon honey
1 teaspoon sesame oil
1 teaspoon vegetable oil
¼ cup (45 g) edamame
½ teaspoon sesame seeds

1 Prepare udon noodles according to package directions, discarding any seasoning packets if included. Drain and rinse under cold running water until noodles are cool.

2 Combine garlic, soy sauce, honey, sesame oil and vegetable oil in a medium bowl.

3 Add the noodles and edamame to the bowl and toss well to coat with sauce.

4 Sprinkle with sesame seeds.

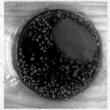

Us IN THIS BENTO
Udon noodles, Underpants,
Unicorn.

OTHER IDEAS FOR U
Uglifruit, Umeboshi, Upside-
down cake, Umbrella,
Underground, Universe,
Up, USA.

V is for Vase

V is another letter with few food options so for this lunch I decided to feature a vase of colorful carrot flowers. Vanilla yogurt with Vs made from grapes is a fun side dish, as are the bright vegetable sticks decorated with cute vehicle picks.

Grapes
2 slices white sandwich bread
Sliced roast beef
Sliced Havarti cheese
Rainbow carrots
Apricot fruit leather
Assorted vegetables such as grape tomatoes, carrots and cucumbers
Vanilla yogurt

EQUIPMENT
Single-tier bento box with two smaller containers
Kitchen shears
Small flower cutters
Decorative picks: flower stems, various vehicles
Large "V"-shaped cutter

Assembly

1 Place the grapes in a single layer covering the bottom of the bento box.

2 Stack the two slices of bread on top of each other. Use the kitchen shears to cut the bread into the shape of a vase. (Cut through both slices at the same time so the two slices are the same size and shape.) Fill the sandwich with the roast beef, cheese and any desired condiments so they fit inside the edges of the bread without showing. You may need to cut or fold the slices so they'll fit.

3 Place the sandwich on top of the grapes with space above the top of the "vase."

4 Cut slices from the thickest end of the carrots. Use cutters to trim the carrot slices into flower shapes. Insert the flower stems into the sides of the carrot flowers. Layer the carrots behind and inside the layers of the sandwich to look like a bouquet.

Variations

If you don't have any picks that resemble flower stems in your bento collection, you can easily swap them out for regular toothpicks or skewers.

5 Cut a large "V" from the fruit leather using the cutter. Layer it on top of the bread "vase."

6 Cut the vegetables into sticks, then stand them on end in one of the smaller side dish containers. They're very pretty if you arrange them in rainbow order. Poke the vehicle picks into the veggies.

7 Spoon vanilla yogurt into the remaining container. Cut a couple of grapes into quarters lengthwise. Place the grape pieces on top of the yogurt in "V" shapes.

Vs IN THIS BENTO
Vase, Vegetables, Vehicles Van, Vanilla yogurt.

OTHER IDEAS FOR V
Vanilla, Veal, Vegemite, Vegetable soup, Venison Vermicelli, Vindaloo, Vinegar, Vest, Vet, Viking, Violin Volcano, Volleyball, Vultures.

W is for Waffles

Chicken and waffles are a classic American combination. Make the chicken lunch box sized by choosing to use wings. Watermelon Ws and winter squash fries are fun accompaniments.

Watermelon
Frozen waffle
Chicken wings, cooked
Maple syrup
Winter Squash "Fries" (see recipe on facing page)

EQUIPMENT
Divided bento box
  (Yumbox Panino)
Decorative picks: whales

Assembly

1 While the squash is cooling, prepare the rest of the lunch: Cut the watermelon into squares about ¼ in. (5 mm) thick. Use a small cutter to cut a few of the squares into W shapes. You can also use a small paring knife for this. Put the watermelon slices in the other side compartment of the bento box and top with the W pieces.

2 Prepare the frozen waffle according to the directions on the package. Allow it to cool to room temperature, then place it in the bento box. Place the chicken wings on top of the waffle.

3 Fill the smallest section of the bento box with some maple syrup. At lunchtime, you can tear the waffle into pieces and dip it in the syrup.

4 Add the Winter Squash "Fries" it to the remaining compartment in the bento box. Decorate it with a couple of whale picks.

Winter Squash "Fries"

I used butternut squash for this recipe, but many other varieties such as acorn or delicata would work just as well. Prep the squash and put it in the oven first, then prepare the rest of the lunch while it's roasting. You can also make the squash the night before to speed up prep time in the morning.

1 medium-sized butternut squash, about 2 lb (900 g)
1–2 tablespoons olive oil
Salt and pepper, to taste

1 Preheat the oven to 400°F (205°C).

2 Cut the squash in half and scoop out the seeds.

3 Peel the skin off and cut the squash into long, thin rectangles (similar to a French fry shape).

4 Toss the squash with the olive oil (the amount you use will depend on how big your squash is).

5 Spread the squash sticks in a single layer on a baking sheet.

6 Roast for about 20 minutes or until the squash is cooked through and golden brown in places.

7 Spread the squash on a paper towel to absorb any excess oil. Allow the squash to cool completely before adding it to the bento box.

Ws IN THIS BENTO
Winter squash, Watermelon, Waffle, Wings, Whale.

OTHER IDEAS FOR W
Wafers, Walnut, Wasabi, Watercress, Wax bean, Wheat bread, White rice, Wild rice, Wontons, Walrus, Water, Windmill, Winter, Wood, Worm.

X is for X-Ray

X is by far and away the most difficult bento box to find items for in this book! There are virtually no foods that start with X in the English language and there are few other words that work for the themes. My solution? Make some X-ray sandwiches and then put lots and lots of Xs in for the side dishes.

X-shaped cookies
Sugar snap peas
Mango
2 slices white bread
Peanut butter or other sandwich
  filling of your choice
Grape fruit leather

EQUIPMENT
Single-tier bento box
Skull and rib cage cutter/stampers
Small, sharp knife
3 silicone baking cups

Assembly

1 Arrange three silicone cups along the long side of the bento box. Fill one with X-shaped cookies (I had to pick through a box of alphabet cookies to get mine.)

2 Trim the sugar snap peas to fit in one of the empty cups. Cut one of the peas in half, lengthwise. Put the peas in the cup and arrange the half peas on top in the shape of an X.

3 Cut the mango into sticks that are the same size as the remaining cup. Arrange two of the sticks in an X shape on top.

Xs IN THIS BENTO
X-ray.

OTHER IDEAS FOR X
Xigua (The Chinese word for watermelon—Yeah, I know it's a stretch. Work with me here!), X Marks the Spot, X-mas, XO, Xylophone.

4 Use the skull and rib cage cutters to cut the bread.

5 Use the same cutters to cut the fruit leather. Leaving the fruit leather on the plastic backing, cut around the outside edges of the shapes you just cut, using a pair of kitchen shears. Press the stamping side of the skeleton cutters into the fruit leather to make an impression of the inner shapes. (The edges will not be sharp enough to cut through.) Use a small sharp knife, to cut the outlines of the skeleton details. Carefully pull the inner area out of the fruit leather, leaving the edges and details on the plastic.

6 Fill the sandwiches with peanut butter, top with the fruit leather cut-outs and place them in the bento box.

Y is for Yeti

A basic gingerbread man cutter does double-duty in this lunch box, molding rice and yams into yeti shapes. A few minutes in a grill pan turns these regular onigiri into yaki onigiri ("grilled rice balls"). Pair them with some yam slices and yellow bell peppers for side dishes.

1 cup (200 g) sushi rice
1 medium yam
Vegetable oil
1 small sheet nori
Yellow bell pepper

EQUIPMENT
Single-tier bento box
Gingerbread man cutter
Small circle cutter
Plastic wrap
Face punch
Decorative waxed paper

Assembly

1 Poke the yam all over with a fork and microwave on high for 8–10 minutes or until the yam is cooked through. (Cooking time is dependent on the size of the yam and your microwave wattage.)

2 When the yam is ready, peel it and cut off a 3 x 3 in. (7.5 x 7.5 cm) chunk. Mash the chunk with a fork. Slice the remaining yam into ½ in. (1 cm) rounds. And arrange them at one end of the bento box.

3 Press a piece of plastic wrap (about 8 in./20.25 cm square) into the gingerbread man cookie cutter. This will make the rice easier to remove when you're done assembling the onigiri.

4 Spread a layer of rice about ⅓ of the depth of the cutter in the bottom of the cutter. Use a small spoon (or your finger) to press it into all the nooks and crannies of the cutter. Spread a thin layer of the mashed yam over the rice. Fill the rest of the space with more rice and press it down firmly into the cutter. Pull the rice out of the cutter using the excess plastic wrap. Repeat to make a second onigiri.

5 Heat a grill pan over medium and brush generously with some vegetable oil. Place the onigiri in the pan and heat until the outside is crisp and brown in places, about 3–4 minutes per side. Remove from the pan and place on a paper towel to absorb any excess oil. Allow to cool.

6 Use the punch to cut faces from the nori. Place nori eyes and nose on each of the onigiri. Then put them in the bento box.

7 Slice the bell pepper into large chunks, then use the circle cutters to cut shapes. Fill in any gaps in the lunch box with the yellow bell pepper circles.

Ys IN THIS BENTO
Yam, Yellow bell pepper,
Yaki onigiri, Yeti.

OTHER IDEAS FOR Y
Yakitori, Yellow squash, Yogurt,
Yolk, Yorkshire pudding,
Yucca, Yacht, Yak, Yard,
Yarn, Yawn, Yell, Yo-yo.

Z is for Zucchini Fritters

Zucchini is the star of this Z bento box, showing up in two forms: savory zucchini fritters and zesty zucchini zeros. Fill the rest of the lunch box with cantaloupe Zs and some cute zoo animal cookies.

ZS IN THIS BENTO

Zucchini, Zigzag, Zoo, Zero.

OTHER IDEAS FOR Z

Ziti, Zucchini bread, Zwieback bread, Zebra, Zeppelin, Zipper.

Zucchini Fritters (see recipe on facing page)
Zucchini
Lemon wedge
Cantaloupe
Zoo animal cookies

EQUIPMENT
Divided bento box (LunchBots Quad)
Decorative zigzag waxed paper
Small circle cutter
Mini circle cutter

Assembly

1 Prepare the Zucchini Fritters. Allow to cool completely. Place a small piece of the waxed paper in one of the compartments, then add 4–5 fritters on top.

2 Cut the zucchini into thin slices. Use the small circle cutter to cut out the middles of the slices, making zero shapes. Use the mini circle cutter to remove the middles from the cut-outs making even smaller zeros.

3 Place the zucchini in a small bowl, and squeeze the lemon wedge over the top. Toss gently to coat, then add the zucchini zeros to the bento box. (Leave any excess lemon juice behind in the bowl.)

4 Cut a ¼ in. (5 mm) slice from the cantaloupe. Use a knife to cut several Zs from the slice (or just use a Z-shaped cutter). Place the scraps in the bottom of one of the bento compartments, then layer the Zs on top.

5 Fill the last section of the bento box with a handful of zoo cookies.

   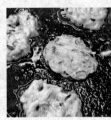 

Zucchini Fritters

2 cups (350 g) spiralized zucchini,
    chopped a bit so it will be easy to scoop
    (or use grated)
1 egg
⅓ cup (45 g) flour
½ teaspoon salt
¼ teaspoon pepper
2 tablespoons parmesan cheese, grated
Olive oil

1 Place the zucchini on a couple of layers of paper towel to absorb any excess moisture.

2 While the zucchini drains, combine the rest of the ingredients in a medium bowl until well mixed. Add the zucchini to the bowl and stir until the wet ingredients completely coat the squash. The batter will be thick.

3 Pour olive oil into a skillet to cover the bottom (about 2 tablespoons). Heat the oil over medium heat until it shimmers.

4 Scoop about two teaspoons of batter and place it in the oil. Flatten the batter out with the back of the scoop. Add more scoops of batter to the pan, but leave plenty of room between each fritter so the oil doesn't cool too much. Sautee for about 3–4 minutes or until the underside of the fritters are set and golden brown.

5 Carefully flip the fritters over and continue to cook until the bottoms are golden and the fritters are cooked all the way through.

6 Remove the fritters from the pan and drain well on a paper towel.

7 Continue to cook in batches of 5 or 6 until you've used all the batter.

NUMBER
BENTOS

Number 1—The Unicorn

I chose the unicorn to represent the number one primarily because of its single horn, but also because the word "one" (or "uni") is right there in the name. And also—kids love unicorns! Of course, a unicorn (in the form of an egg here) needs a rainbow to go with it, so I included an array of veggies in bright colors along with a rainbow cereal treat.

Hard-boiled egg
Purple carrots
Cherry tomatoes
Orange carrots
Yellow pepper strips
Sugar snap peas
Rainbow fruit cereal
Fruit leather

EQUIPMENT
Single-tier bento box
Black food-safe marker
2 round pink silicone
  baking cup
Medium "1" cutter

Assembly

1 First make the unicorn egg: Peel the hard-boiled egg. Cut a thin slice from one of the purple carrots (about ⅛ in./2–3 mm thick and 2 in./5 cm long). Cut the carrot in half round the edges with a paring knife and found the edges so it looks like a horse's mane. Use the knife to cut a thin slit from top to bottom on the hard-boiled egg. The slit should be slightly narrower than the width of the strip of carrot "mane." Wedge the carrot into the slit.

2 Cut a long, thin triangle from the other half of the carrot piece for the unicorn horn. Poke a hole near the top of the egg opposite the mane and poke the wider end of the food-safe pen into the egg. Use the food safe pen to draw a unicorn face—eyes, ears and nostrils—on the egg below the horn. Put the unicorn egg into one of the silicone cups and place it in a corner of the bento box.

3 Fill the other silicone cup with a handful of rainbow cereal. Place the cup in the corner opposite the unicorn.

4 Slice the vegetables to the desired sizes, then arrange them in stripes going across the bento box from left to right—red, orange, yellow, green, purple.

5 Use the 1 cutter to cut a shape from the fruit leather.

Tip
If you are having trouble getting a clean cut through the fruit leather, flip it over along with the cutter, then press firmly on the plastic backing along the edge of the cutter with your finger.

Number 2—A Pair of Mittens

The main part of this lunch—a pair of mittens—is pretty tame and I've paired it with a couple of oranges and some cucumber sticks for decorum's sake. But here's the thing: when I asked the kids I know what they think of when they hear "number two" they all laughed and said the same thing: poop! I knew I had to include a bit of toilet humor in this lunch so I packed some chocolate yogurt with sprinkles shaped like the poop emoji. If that's too much for you, feel free to leave the poop sprinkles off or skip the yogurt altogether. If you can't find poop sprinkles you can substitute chocolate chips or other small chocolate candies.

2 clementines
Cucumber
Chocolate-flavored yogurt
2 slices white sandwich bread
Peanut butter

EQUIPMENT
Two-tier bento box with
  lidded inner container
  (EcoLunchboxes 3-in-1)
2 glasses decorative picks
Small "2" cutter
Poop emoji sprinkles or
  candies
Medium mitten cutter
Rainbow sprinkles

Assembly

1 Poke the glasses picks into the clementines and place them to the side of the lidded container inside the bento box.

2 Cut a chunk of the cucumber the same height as the bento box. Use a knife to peel the cucumber by cutting around the edge. Cut the cucumber into long sticks and place them on the other side of the lidded container. Cue a few 2s from the cucumber skin with the cutter and place them on top of the cucumber sticks.

3 Fill the inner container with the chocolate yogurt, stirring to combine the yogurt and the chocolate if necessary. Sprinkle with the poop emoji candies. Don't forget to put the lid on top of the container!

Variation

If your child isn't a fan of peanut butter (or if it's not allowed in your school to support kids with allergies) you can substitute another nut butter, sunflower seed butter or ever cream cheese.

Tip

Some children are more adept at peeling oranges than others. If your child struggles with the task make it easier for them by making a small cut in a hidden part of the oranges to get him started.

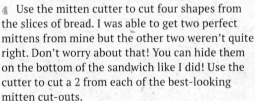

4   Use the mitten cutter to cut four shapes from the slices of bread. I was able to get two perfect mittens from mine but the other two weren't quite right. Don't worry about that! You can hide them on the bottom of the sandwich like I did! Use the cutter to cut a 2 from each of the best-looking mitten cut-outs.

5   Spread peanut butter on the mittens without the twos and then place the other bread pieces on top.

6   Put some of the rainbow sprinkles inside the 2 cut-outs. The sprinkles should stick to the peanut butter but if they don't, press them gently into the peanut butter with the tip of your finger.

7   Spread a thin layer of peanut butter on the bottom of each mitten sandwich.

8   Pour some sprinkles on a plate and then dip the peanut butter stripe into the sprinkles. The sprinkles should stick to the peanut butter giving it a brightly colored "cuff."

9   Put the sandwiches in the second layer of the bento box.

Tip

Pouring the sprinkles out on a plate and dipping the sandwich instead of pouring them onto the sandwich accomplishes two things: **1** The sprinkles don't fly all over the counter and make a big mess, and **2** You can pour the sprinkles back into their container afterward and minimize waste.

Number 3—Triangles

Three is the magic number! I filled this lunch with triangles, stoplights and the number 3 itself—all in multiples of three.

Celery stalks
Cream cheese
Red, yellow and green bell pepper
Mini pita rounds
Strawberries
Mango

EQUIPMENT
Divided bento box (EasyLunchboxes)
Mini circle cutter
Small "3" cutter

Assembly

1 Cut the celery stalks into lengths that will fit in one of the side compartments of the bento box. Fill three of the celery sticks with cream cheese. Place the remaining sticks into the bento box.

2 Cut three small circles from each color of the bell pepper chunks. Poke the circles into the cream cheese on the three filled celery sticks with the red circles on top, the yellow in the middle and the green on the bottom. Put the stoplight celery on top of the plain celery in the bento box.

3 Spread a thin layer of cream cheese on each of the pitas. Thinly slice a couple of strawberries and layer on one of the pitas. Top with the other pita, then cut into three equal wedges. Place the sandwich in the largest compartment of the bento box. Garnish with one of the tips of the strawberries (if you haven't already used them all.

4 Cut a chunk off one side of the mango. Scoop the flesh of the mango out of the skin with a large spoon. Cut a thin slice from the mango and use the cutter to cut three 3s from the slice. Cut the remaining mango into three chunks and add it to the bento box. Top each chunk with one of the mango 3s.

Tip

Sometimes kids aren't fans of celery because of the stringy fibers that are part of its structure. I've found that if you pull some of those fibers off before giving it to them they are more likely to eat it. To remove the fibers, slip a knife under the outside edge of the celery stalk, pull up a bit and then gently peel the fibers off the length of the vegetable. Repeat as necessary to get most of the stringy bits off.

Variation

You can substitute fruit circles for the peppers on the stoplights if you prefer. Strawberry, mango and kiwi would work just as well.

Number 4 — The Four Seasons

The four seasons affect so much of our day-to-day lives that it felt natural to make them the centerpiece of this bento box. It really doesn't matter what kind of sandwich you make here but it is nice to be able to put the cheese scraps inside the sandwich to avoid wasting them. If your sandwich doesn't go well with cheese, just have the scraps for a snack while you make the lunch!

Slices of whole wheat sandwich
  bread
Sandwich fillings and condiments
  of your choice (I used turkey,
  Havarti and mayo)
Sliced cheddar cheese
Sliced Havarti cheese
4 cherry tomatoes
4 small strawberries
4 chocolate covered raisins

EQUIPMENT
Divided bento box (Yumbox Panino)
Stamping cutters—daisy, sun,
  leaf and snowflake
Mini circle cutter
Small "4" cutter
4 decorative eye picks

Assembly

1 Assemble a sandwich on wheat bread with the fillings and condiments of your choice. Trim the crusts off the edges of the sandwich to form a rectangle shape. Cut the sandwich in half lengthwise, then again in half widthwise to create four smaller rectangles. Place the mini sandwiches in the largest section of the bento box.

2 Use the cutters to stamp the shapes out of the cheese. Cut the daisy and the snowflake from the Havarti cheese. Cut the sun and the leaf from the cheddar cheese. Cut a small circle from the cheddar and place it in the center of the daisy. Put each of the cheese shapes on one of the sandwiches.

3 Put the four cherry tomatoes in one of the smaller sections of the bento box. Cut a 4 shape from the Havarti with the cutter and place that shape on top of the tomatoes.

4 Trim the tops off the strawberries, then insert the eye picks into the sides of the berries. Put them in the other side dish section in the bento box.

5 Add four chocolate covered raisins to the small snack compartment in the lunch box.

Number 5—Stars

Stars are a great way to represent the number five and they make this lunch fun. I used some of my star cutters to cut cheese and kiwis, but you could use them on almost any food you can think of! I also chose to include five skewers with five items on each one and five slices of tomato. And the lunch is finished off by a 5 cheese cut-out.

½ in (1.25 cm) slice cheddar
  cheese (cut from a block)
¼ in (5 mm) slice cheddar
  cheese (also cut from a block)
1 kiwi
1 or 2 medium tomatoes
1 fully cooked chicken
  apple sausage
Red apple
Whole wheat pretzel sticks

EQUIPMENT
Divided bento box (LunchBots Cinco)
Small star cutter
Medium star cutter
Medium "5" cutter
3 round silicone baking cups
5 decorative skewers

Assembly

1 Put a silicone cup into each of the smaller sections of the bento box.

2 Use the small star cutter to cut five stars from the thicker slice of cheese. Put them inside one of the silicone cups.

3 Cut the ends off the kiwi, then cut it in half. Slide a spoon around the inside edge of the skin to separate it from the kiwi's flesh. Cut the kiwi into 5 slices, then use the medium and small star cutters to cut them into star shapes. Add the kiwi slices to a silicone cup.

4 Slice the tomato into five slices and add to the last silicone cup.

5 Slice the sausage into 12 equal rounds. Cut the apple into 13 1-in. (2.5-cm) chunks (you will have apple leftover). Thread the sausage and apple chunks onto the skewers alternating chunks of meat and fruit. If you want the chunks to come out even make three skewers with three apples and two sausage and two skewers with two apples and three sausages. Add the skewers to the lunch box.

6 Fill the remaining compartment with a layer of the pretzel sticks.

7 Cut a 5 shape from the thinner slice of cheese using the cutter.

Number 6—Garden

This lunch has a loose garden theme—a six-legged ant, 6 butterfly-shaped crackers, 6 stalks of asparagus "grass" and 6 ham rosebuds. I also included a yummy treat of bananas with chocolate hummus. If you've never had chocolate hummus before, it's very similar to Nutella or other chocolate spreads but with an added boost of protein from the chickpeas it's made from. If you can't find chocolate hummus, just substitute Nutella or peanut butter.

Avocado
Banana
Chocolate hummus (or Nutella)
6 pretzel crackers
Edamame hummus
3 black olives
6 thin stalks of asparagus
2 slices deli ham

EQUIPMENT
Divided bento box (LunchBots
   Snack Tray)
"6"-shaped sprinkles
2 silicone baking cups
Leaf decorative picks

Assembly

1 Cut the ends of a banana and then slice it into 6 equal chunks (about ¾-1 in./2–2.5 cm wide).

2 Divide the bananas between two of the compartments in the bento box.

3 Spread a little bit of the chocolate hummus on the exposed ends of the bananas, then add a few of the 6-shaped sprinkles to the top.

4 Put a silicone cup in one of the compartments, then fill it with the pretzel crackers.

5 Fill the other silicone cup with the edamame hummus.

6 Make an olive "ant": cut the olives in half from top to bottom. Place three of the halves on top of the edamame hummus end to end. Slice the other halves of the olives cross-wise into six thin slices. Arrange them next to the middle olive on the hummus to look like legs.

7 Cut the asparagus into 2-in. (5-cm) lengths. Microwave them in a bowl with a little water for about 30 seconds or until they are just barely tender. Add them to the bento box.

Tip

Concerned about bananas turning brown in the lunch box? If you prevent the cut ends of the fruit from being exposed to the air, the peels might brown a bit, but the flesh will be fine. Here, I pressed one side of the banana chunks against the lunch box and I covered the other end with chocolate hummus. They were fresh hours later!

8 Slice the ham into strips about 1 in. (2.5 cm) thick. Roll the ham into six spirals (double up layers of the ham if you have more than six strips). Spear the ham with the leaf picks and add them to the last section of the bento box.

Number 7—Days of the Week

Every week has seven days, so this lunch includes a mini calendar spelling them out. I also made a seven petal flower by creating a ring of cantaloupe circles. There are seven meatballs for a bit of protein and seven green beans for some greenery.

7 mini meatballs
7 green beans
Sliced gouda cheese
Small square crackers (such as Wheat Thins)
Cantaloupe
7 blueberries
7 small bunny crackers

EQUIPMENT
Divided bento box (PlanetBox Rover)
Small circle cutter
Small alphabet cutters—"M," "T," "W," "F" and "S"
Medium "7"-shaped cutter

Assembly

1 Place the mini meatballs in one of the sections of the lunch box. Top with the cheese 7.

2 Lightly steam the green beans by microwaving them in a bowl with a little water for about 4 minutes or until just tender. Trim the green beans to the length of one of the compartments and add to the bento box.

3 Use the 7 cutter to cut a shape from the cheese. Put the 7 on top of the green beans.

4 Use the letter cutters to cut the cheese into one M, two Ts, one W, one F and two Ss.

5 Place a few layers of crackers in the longest section of the bento box.

6 Arrange the letters on the crackers in order to represent the days of the week: M, T, W, T, F, S, S.

7 Cut a ½ in. (1 cm) slice of cantaloupe. Use the small circle cutter to cut seven circle shapes from the melon.

8 Arrange the melon circles into a circle in the largest compartment of the bento box. Fill the center of the circle with the blueberries.

9 Place the bunny crackers in the smallest compartment in the box.

Number 8—Spider

The figure eight pastries in this lunch are delicious as well as being a fun shape. I chose prosciutto to twist into them because of its dry texture. If the flavor is too strong for your child, you can use regular ham but be sure to blot off any excess moisture so the pastries aren't soggy. I added a few more eights to this bento in the form of a friendly spider and tomatoes that are threaded onto skewers to look like eights.

One 14 oz (400 g) package refrigerated pizza
  dough
4 slices prosciutto
1 tablespoon grated parmesan cheese
Grape tomatoes
Blackberries

EQUIPMENT
Divided bento box (EasyLunchboxes)
Decorative waxed paper (optional)
Crab and flower decorative picks
Spider-shaped silicone cup
Icing googly eyes

Assembly

1 Preheat the oven to 400°F (205°C).

2 Roll the pizza dough out on a cutting board and slice it into 12 strips approximately 1 in. (2.5 cm) wide.

3 Cut the prosciutto slices lengthwise into 3 strips.

4 Place a piece of the prosciutto on top of each of the dough strips.

5 Twist the dough strips, form into figure eights and place on an ungreased cookie sheet.

6 Brush the dough lightly with a bit of olive oil and sprinkle with the parmesan cheese.

7 Bake for 8 minutes or until the eights are golden brown.

8 Allow to cool, then add to the bento box.

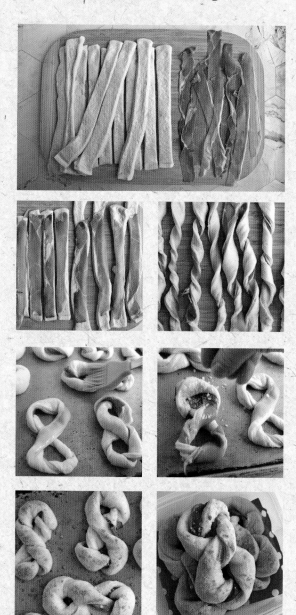

9 Thread two tomatoes onto each of the picks to form an 8 shape. Put a few more tomatoes into one of the side compartments in the bento box and place the picks on top.

10 Fill the spider cup with blackberries. Arrange 8 icing googly eyes on top of the berries. Put the cup in the remaining empty section of the bento box.

Number 9—Baseball

My kids have played baseball for years, so when I started brainstorming lunch ideas for the number nine, baseball immediately sprang to mind—9 players on the field, 9 innings in a game! The carrot baseball bats look complicated but they are pretty easy to make with a few cuts of a knife. Pocket sandwiches like the baseball in this lunch are fun to make and my kids have always enjoyed eating them. You can fill them with any soft fillings (tuna salad, PB&J) as long as you don't go overboard with the amount. And be aware that anything too hard or too thick can tear the bread.

1 hard-boiled egg
2 teaspoons mayonnaise
2 slices white sandwich bread
5 baby carrot sticks
Blueberries
Chicago mix popcorn (caramel and
   cheddar mix)

EQUIPMENT
Divided bento box (PlanetBox Rover)
4 in. (10 cm) empanada press
Red food-safe marker
Decorative picks: baseballs
Baseball and bat sprinkles
"9"-shaped sprinkles

Assembly

1 Chop the egg into a small dice, then mix it together with the mayo and salt and pepper to taste.

2 Use the cutting side of the empanada press to cut two circles from the bread slices.

3 Put the egg salad in the middle of one of the circles. Top with the other circle of bread. Open the empanada cutter, place it fluted-side down on top of the sandwich and press down firmly to seal the sandwich. Trim any excess bread off the fluted edge to make the sandwich look neater.

4 Add curved stitching lines to the top of the sandwich with the red food coloring marker.

5 Add decorative grass sheets to the largest compartment of the bento box. Top with the sandwich.

6 Cut the carrots in half. Use a paring knife to cut a small triangle from each long side to resemble a baseball bat. Arrange nine of the carrot halves in the long compartment of the bento box. (You can eat the 10th one for a little snack. You deserve it!)

7 Add a handful of popcorn to one of the remaining compartments in the lunch box. Top with the baseball and bat sprinkles.

8 Fill the fourth compartment with blue-berries. Add the baseball picks.

9 Fill the treat compartment with some of the 9 sprinkles.

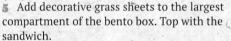

Tip
Look for ways your supplies can do double-duty. For this lunch I used the same sprinkles that appear in the "6" bento box—I just turned them upside down!

Number 10—Bowling

A classic roast beef sandwich with all the fixings headlines this ten lunch. Most of the work for this one goes into cutting the bowling pins, but it goes pretty quickly once you get started. Arrange them on top of the sandwich with an olive for a bowling ball and you'll score a strike!

2 slices whole wheat sandwich bread
Sandwich fillings: roast beef, Swiss
   cheese, lettuce and condiments
   (or other fillings of your choice)
2 slices of muenster cheese
Black olive
Lettuce
2 or 3 grape tomatoes
10 freeze-dried strawberries

EQUIPMENT
Divided bento box (EasyLunchboxes)
Red food-safe marker
Toothpick
Small "1" and "0" cutters

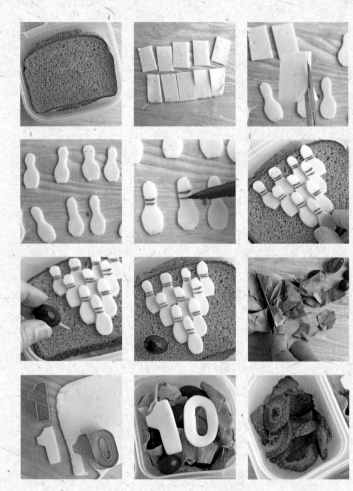

Assembly

1 Make a sandwich using the roast beef, cheese, lettuce and condiments. Add it to the bento box.

2 Cut a slice of the muenster cheese into 10 equal-sized rectangles. Use a paring knife or kitchen scissors to cut the rectangles in bowling pin shapes.

3 Add two stripes of red to each of the pins using a red food-safe marker.

4 Arrange the cheese pins on top of the sandwich in a triangle shape: four at the top of the sandwich, three overlapping the first row, two more overlapping the second row and one pin at the bottom.

5 Spear the olive onto the end of the toothpick, then poke it into the sandwich.

6 Cut the lettuce into strips and add it to one of the side compartments. Top with the grape tomatoes.

7 Cut a 1 and a 0 from the other slice of the muenster cheese. Add them on top of the salad.

8 Place the freeze-dried strawberries in the last section of the bento box.

COLOR
BENTOS

White Bento Box

An all-white bento box is easy to pack for most young kids because white foods tend to be the foods they like the most. What's *not* easy is finding white fruits and veggies that they'll enjoy because there simply aren't very many options to choose from. If your child isn't familiar with jicama, it might be worth trying it out on her. The crisp, slightly sweet flesh is reminiscent of carrot and mild enough that even picky eaters can enjoy it.

2 slices of white
  sandwich bread
Sliced deli turkey
Sliced Havarti cheese
Condiments—mayo,
  mustard, etc.
Jicama
Banana

EQUIPMENT
Single-tier bento box
  with a divider
Large snowflake cutter
Mini diamond or triangle
  shaped cutter
White baking cup
Decorative picks—
  white seal and bunnies

Assembly

1 Use the large cutter to cut two snowflakes from the sliced bread. (Save the leftover scraps for another use.) Use the mini cutter to cut six more holes from one of the slices of bread to make a more intricate snowflake for the top of the sandwich.

2 Cut the turkey and cheese with the snowflake cutter. Add condiments to the bottom piece of bread, then top with the cut turkey slice. Arrange any scraps of turkey and cheese on top so they don't hang over the edge of the sandwich, then top with the cheese snowflake. Close the sandwich and add to the bento box. Add the divider to the box.

3 Fill the empty space around the sandwich with popcorn.

4 Dice the jicama. Add it to the white baking cup and place it in the bento box.

5 Peel the banana and cut it in half. Add it to the remaining space in the box.

6 Insert the seal and bunny picks in the jicama and banana chunks.

Variation

I used Havarti cheese for the sandwich in this lunch box because I've found most kids like it's mild flavor. You could substitute Swiss, muenster or sliced mozzarella if you prefer.

Pink Bento Box

We start our trip through the bento box rainbow with this pretty pink lunch. I made two cups of sushi rice for this lunch so you can use an entire packet of the pink food coloring at once. It makes more rice than you need for a single lunch but any leftovers can be frozen for later use. Natural pink food coloring can be purchased at natural food stores or online.

2 cups (250 g) sushi rice
½ teaspoon natural pink food coloring powder (1 packet)
2 tablespoons rice wine vinegar
1 tablespoon sugar
1 teaspoon salt
½ cup (60 g) cooked, peeled shrimp (frozen is fine)
½ in. (1.25 cm) thick slice watermelon
Small pink crackers

EQUIPMENT
Single-tier bento box
Two tablespoon cookie scoop
Plastic wrap
3 small pink silicone cups
2 pink heart decorative picks
Small flower-shaped plunger cutter
1 small pink sheep-shaped silicone cup

Assembly

1 Prepare sushi rice according to package directions, adding the pink food coloring to the water before cooking. The water will be a very bright pink color at first, but the color will mellow as it cooks.

2 Combine vinegar, sugar and salt in a small bowl. Stir until the salt and sugar are mostly dissolved. When rice finishes cooking, stir in the vinegar mixture. Spread rice on a plate to cool.

3 Once rice is cool enough to handle, use the cookie scoop to pick up a portion of rice and place it on a small piece of plastic wrap. Gather the corners of the plastic wrap together and twist them around the rice to shape it into a ball (see photo). Unwrap the ball and set it into one of the small round silicone cups. Repeat to fill

the rest of the cups, then place them in a diagonal line across the bento box.

4 Spear a few of the shrimp with the decorative picks. Place the remaining shrimp in the corner of the bento box sectioned off by the rice. Place the skewered shrimp on top.

5 Use the flower cutter to cut six pieces of watermelon, pressing firmly on the plunger to stamp the image into the top of each piece. Line the watermelon flowers up next to the rice in the bento box.

6 Add the sheep cup to the remaining space in the bento box and fill it with the crackers.

PINK FOODS USED IN THIS BENTO
Colored rice, Shrimp, Watermelon, Pink crackers.

OTHER IDEAS FOR PINK FOODS
Ham, Hot dog, Salmon, Pink grapefruit, Cara Cara oranges, Radishes, Dragon fruit, Pink lady apples, Pickled ginger.

Red Bento Box

It's easy to find bright red foods at the market, so this rosy red box can be filled with healthy produce without too much trouble. If you want to be a little more daring, try swapping the raspberries or tomatoes with less common blood oranges or pomegranate seeds.

Raspberries
Dried cranberries
Beet chips
Sliced salami
Grape tomatoes
Red bell pepper
Red apple

EQUIPMENT
Divided bento box
  (Yumbox Panino)
Red robot cupcake
  decoration
2 red round silicone
  baking cups
Red crayon decorative
  pick
Small heart-shaped cutter
Small sharp paring knife
  or craft knife

Assembly

1 Place raspberries in one of the medium sections of the bento box. Top with the red robot decoration.

2 Add cranberries to the smallest compartment.

3 Place a red cup in the corner of the largest compartment of the lunch box. Fill with beet chips.

4 Fold salami slices in half, and then into quarters (see photos). Add them to the remaining red cup with the point side down until the cup is full. The salami should have a ruffled appearance. Add the cup to the large compartment of the lunch box, opposite the chips.

5 Thread a few tomatoes onto the decorative crayon pick. Fill one of the empty spaces in the large section of the bento box with some more tomatoes and then top with the pick.

6 Cut a large slice off the side of the red pepper. Use the cutter to make two or three heart shapes. Chop the rest of the pepper into bite-sized pieces and fill the rest of the empty space in the large section of the bento box. Add the heart-shaped pieces on top.

> ### *Tip*
> This is a job for grown-ups! Go slowly when you first start removing the skin and be careful not to cut yourself with the knife. As you get used to the technique you will get faster at it—I promise!

7 Cut a large piece off the side of the apple, then trim it to fit in the remaining empty compartment in the lunch box. Use the knife to score the skin of the apple in a triangle pattern (see photos). Be careful that you don't cut too far down into the flesh of the apple! Your goal should be to only cut through the skin.

8 Gently slide the tip of the knife under one of the triangles you've cut into the apple's skin. Keep the knife parallel to the flesh of the apple as much as possible and slide it around the edges of the triangle until the skin pops off. Continue removing every other triangle of skin from the apple until the entire surface is covered with the pattern. If brown apples bother you or your child, sprinkle a little bit of Fruit Fresh powder on the top of your design to preserve the white color.

9 Cut some more slices of apple and place at the bottom of the apple compartment. Top with the decorated piece of apple.

RED FOODS USED IN THIS BENTO

Raspberries, Dried cranberries, Beet chips, Sliced salami, Grape tomatoes, Red bell pepper, Red apple.

OTHER IDEAS FOR RED FOODS

Cherries, Strawberries, Watermelon, Pomegranate seeds, Ruby red grapefruit, Blood oranges, Radish, Beet crackers, Red fish crackers.

Orange Bento Box

Not only are orange foods bright and pretty—their natural sweetness is appealing to kids! I used frozen butternut squash cubes for convenience, but if you have fresh squash cubes you can roast them at 400°F (205°C) for about 15–20 minutes while you assemble the rest of the lunch.

¼ cup (30 g) cooked short grain rice, cooled
⅓ cup (40 g) Apricot Chicken (see recipe on facing page)
½ cup (60 g) frozen, cubed butternut squash
Cinnamon sugar, to taste
1 medium orange
1 carrot, 1–1½ in. (2–4 cm) wide at the end

EQUIPMENT
Divided bento box (LunchBots Quad)
Medium circle cutter
Small star cutter
Orange silicone baking cup
2 orange flower decorative picks

Assembly

1 Layer rice in the bottom of one bento box compartment.

2 Spoon Apricot Chicken on top of rice.

3 Toss roasted squash with cinnamon sugar, put it in the orange silicone cup and place in a second compartment of the lunch box.

4 Cut four slices of orange. Put two slices in the bottom of a compartment, then put two more slices on top of them with round edges together.

5 Cut a slice of the orange peel. Use the circle cutter to cut it into a lens (pointed oval) shape (as shown). Insert the two flower picks on either side of one of the pointed ends. Place on top of the orange slices to make a butterfly.

ORANGE FOODS USED IN THIS BENTO
Apricot jam, Orange slices, Carrot, Butternut squash.

OTHER IDEAS FOR ORANGE FOODS
Acorn squash, Apricot, Cantaloupe, Cheddar cheese, Dried apricots, Kabocha squash, Mango, Orange pepper, Nectarine, Peach, Persimmon, Pumpkin, Sweet potato.

6 Peel the carrot and trim the ends. Cut 6 thin slices from the wide end of the carrot. Cut stars from the carrot slices using the small star cutter. Cut the rest of the carrot into sticks and place in the fourth compartment in the bento box. Layer the carrot stars on top.

Apricot Chicken

This delectably sweet apricot chicken comes together very quickly when you use rotisserie chicken or leftovers from dinner the night before. No need to be fussy about which cut you use—white or dark meat works equally well.

1 tablespoon apricot preserves
½ teaspoon soy sauce
⅓ cup (40 g) chopped, cooked chicken

Stir preserves and soy sauce together in a bowl until blended. Add chicken and toss to coat.

Yellow Bento Box

This sunny bento will bring a smile to anyone's face. The tamagoyaki (rolled omelet) has just a touch of sugar in it, which reminds me of a dessert custard. Yellow cauliflower can be found in many well-stocked supermarkets.

6 pieces Tamagoyaki (see recipe on facing page)
Frozen corn, thawed
Pineapple chunks
Dried banana chips
Yellow bell pepper
Small yellow tomatoes
Yellow cauliflower

EQUIPMENT
Two-tier stacking bento box
Medium yellow silicone baking cup
Large yellow silicone cup
Small yellow silicone cup
Medium star cutter
Small giraffe cutter
Assorted yellow decorative picks

Assembly

1 Spoon the corn into the medium silicone cup and set it in one end of one of the layers of the bento box.

2 Add the pineapple to the large cup and banana chips to the small cup and put them in the other layer of the box. Fill the empty spaces between the pineapple and banana chips with tomatoes and pieces of cauliflower.

3 Cut two slices from the bell pepper. Use the star cutter to cut a star from one of the slices.

4 Cut several small giraffe shapes from the other slice.

5 Add the Tamagoyaki pieces to the empty space above the corn.

6 Top the egg with the pepper giraffes and the corn with the pepper star.

7 Add several decorative picks to the pineapple and vegetables.

YELLOW FOODS USED IN THIS BENTO

Egg, Corn, Pineapple, Banana chips, Yellow pepper, Yellow tomatoes, Yellow cauliflower.

OTHER IDEAS FOR YELLOW FOODS

Applesauce, Apples, Banana (fresh), Lemon, Mango, Mustard, Pear, Polenta, Quince, Star fruit (carambola), Turmeric (used as a seasoning), Wax beans, Yellow dragonfruit, Yellow summer squash, Yellow watermelon.

Tamagoyaki (Pan-fried Rolled Omelet)

2 eggs
1 teaspoon sugar
2 teaspoons mirin
1 teaspoon vegetable oil

1 Beat two eggs in a small bowl.

2 Stir together sugar and mirin until sugar dissolves. Add to egg and give it another stir.

3 Heat oil in a small non-stick skillet over medium low heat. Wipe excess oil out of pan with a paper towel.

4 Pour in just enough egg to cover the bottom of the pan completely (about ½ of the mixture).

5 When the top of the egg is mostly set, carefully roll it into a cylinder, then slide it back to the side of the pan where you started rolling.

6 Pour the remaining egg mixture into the pan, then lift the side of the omelet and tilt the pan so some of the egg runs underneath it. Let the omelet drop back in the pan.

7 When the top of the egg is mostly set, roll the egg up the rest of the way.

8 Remove the omelet from the pan and place on a sushi rolling mat. Roll the omelet up in the mat and place it on top of a bowl or a rack to cool. (The sushi mat helps preserve the round shape.) You can put it in the refrigerator to speed this step up while you make the rest of the lunch.

9 Once the omelet is cool, slice into rounds.

Green Bento Box

There are so many delicious green foods that it's simple to make an all-green bento box. The hardest part is choosing what you want to put in it and leaving some favorites behind. For this lunch I packed green roll-up sandwiches, a variety of fruits and veggies and some green chili tortilla chips for a bit of crunch.

Large spinach tortilla
2 tablespoons guacamole
1 or 2 lettuce leaves
2 slices deli turkey
Cucumber sticks
Honeydew melon balls (see sidebar)
Sugar snap peas
Celery
Green chili tortilla chips

EQUIPMENT
Single-tier bento box
Large green silicone cup
Green robot cupcake decoration
Green crayon decorative pick

Assembly

1 Lay the tortilla out on a cutting board and spread a thin layer of guacamole over the top. Spread the lettuce leaves evenly over the guacamole and then top with the turkey slices. Lay the cucumber sticks along the bottom of the tortilla and then tightly roll up the tortilla.

2 Slice the tortilla roll into 1-in. (2.5-cm) thick slices. Stack them in one end of the bento box.

GREEN FOODS USED IN THIS BENTO

Spinach tortilla, Guacamole, Cucumber, Honeydew melon, Sugar snap peas, Celery, Green tortilla chips.

OTHER IDEAS FOR GREEN FOODS

Artichoke, Asparagus, Avocado, Broccoli, Brussels sprouts, Edamame, Green apple, Green beans, Green grapes, Green olives, Green pepper, Peas, Pickles, Zucchini.

3 Place the large cup at the other end of the bento box and fill with the melon balls. (See sidebar.) Add the green crayon pick to one of the melon balls.

4 Trim the snap peas and celery sticks to the height of the bento box. Stand the snap peas and celery sticks on end around the cup holding the melon balls.

5 Fill the remaining space in the bento box with the tortilla chips. Add the robot cupcake decoration on top of the chips.

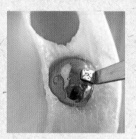
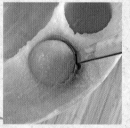

Green Melon Balls

Making melon balls isn't tricky—as long as you know how. If you don't know the basics of how to get perfectly round balls, it can be frustrating to find yourself scooping hemispheres. Here are a few tips to get perfect melon balls every time:

1 Start with the right tool. It's easiest if you buy a dedicated melon baller. If you don't have one, round metal measuring spoons can work too.

2 Insert the melon baller into the melon at an angle. Press it firmly down into the melon until the hole in the top is touching the fruit. You will also see juice coming out of the hole at this point.

3 Twist the melon baller to form the ball.

4 Once the melon baller has flipped a full 180 degrees, pop the melon ball out of the fruit.

Variation
You can swap pesto for the guacamole in the roll-up sandwiches for a different, but equally delicious flavor.

Blue Bento Box

Blue foods are extremely rare in nature, so you need to get a little creative to make an all-blue bento lunch! To solve this problem, I dyed some white foods (rice noodles and tofu) with food coloring to make a simple noodle dish. Of course, blueberries had to go into this bento box and I finished it off with some blue candies and blue jello that I made right in the bento box. Be sure to prepare the jello the night before so it has the necessary time to set up.

Blue gelatin dessert mix (such as Jell-o Berry
  Blue flavor)
Gummi sharks
Blue Rice Noodle and Tofu Salad
1 tablespoon soy sauce
1½ teaspoons toated sesame oil
½ teaspoon granulated sugar
1 small clove garlic, crushed
Blueberries
Blue candies

EQUIPMENT
Divided bento box (Yumbox Panino)
Blue decorative picks: dolphins and whale

Assembly

1 The night before you are going to send the bento box, prepare the gelatin dessert according to package directions.

2 Put two gummi sharks into one of the side sections of the bento box. Pour gelatin over the candies to cover. (It looks really cool if you can manage to have the fins on the candies sticking out above the top of the gelatin.) Close the bento box and put it in the refrigerator overnight so it has time to set.

3 Add the Blue Rice Noodle and Tofu Salad to the main compartment of the bento box.

4 Mix the soy sauce, sesame oil, sugar and garlic together in a small bowl. Pour into a small jar or container. Pack the sauce into the bento box, or just place it in the lunch bag to pour over the noodles at lunchtime.

5 Put the blueberries in the empty side compartment. Poke the picks into a few of the berries.

6 Add the blue candies to the smallest compartment.

BLUE FOODS USED IN THIS BENTO
Blueberries, Blue jello, Blue candies.

OTHER IDEAS FOR BLUE FOODS
That's it.
I used them all!

Tip
I strongly prefer a gel food coloring for this recipe. I tried using natural blue food dye to color the rice noodles and tofu but it doesn't provide enough vibrancy to make them look blue. No matter how long I soaked them, they ended up an unappetizing pale bluish gray color.

Blue Rice Noodle and Tofu Salad

3 oz (80 g) rice noodles
4 oz (120 g) firm tofu
Blue gel food coloring
1 teaspoon toasted sesame oil
1 tablespoon carrot, grated
2 tablespoons red cabbage, grated
1 tablespoon vegetable oil

1 Put noodles in a large dish and cover with water to soak them.

2 Cut the tofu into two slices about ½-in. (1.25-cm) thick. Place on a few layers of paper towel, put another paper towel on top and then put the dish with the noodles and water on top of that. Let stand while the water for cooking the noodles comes to a boil. (This step helps squeeze as much moisture as possible out of the tofu, which then allows it to absorb more of the blue dye.)

3 Bring about 1 quart of water to a boil in a large saucepan. Turn off the stove and add blue gel food coloring one drop at a time until the water is a strong blue color. (The specific amount will vary depending on what type and brand of food coloring you use.) Add the pre-soaked rice noodles to the pot and let them sit in the hot water for about 5 minutes (or the amount of time specified on the package.)

4 While the noodles are cooking, fill a dish with water and add a few drops of food coloring until it's a strong blue color. Cut the tofu into cubes and soak in the blue water while you finish preparing the noodles.

5 Drain the noodles well but DON'T rinse them. Put the noodles in a large bowl and toss them with a teaspoon of sesame oil. Allow to cool.

6 Add the carrots and cabbage to the bowl and toss.

7 Remove the tofu from the dye and drain well on paper towels.

8 Heat the vegetable oil over medium heat. Add the tofu and sauté until golden brown in spots.

9 Cool and toss with the noodle mixture.

Purple Bento Box

Besides being beautiful, the cabbage-based salad in this lunch box is crunchy with a load of sweetness from the dried cherries and the raspberry vinaigrette. The beet hummus is a great accompaniment for the cauliflower and my kids really enjoy it. Fill the rest of the lunch with familiar fruits for a purple-licious meal.

Beet hummus
Purple Salad (see recipe on facing paper)
Purple cauliflower
Plum
Red grapes

EQUIPMENT
Divided bento box (Lunchbots Cinco)
Small container with lid
Purple silicone baking cup
Decorative picks: purple crayons
 and purple koala

Assembly

1 Prepare Purple Salad and add it to one of the larger compartments in the bento box.

2 Fill the small container with the beet hummus and add it to a smaller section.

3 Cut the cauliflower into bite-sized pieces and add them to the other large section of the bento.

4 Pit the plum and cut it into bite-sized chunks. Add it to the bento box. Spear the crayon pick into one of the chunks.

5 Put the purple cup in the remaining compartment. Fill it with grapes and then add the koala pick.

Tip Purple carrots are usually found in multicolored packs of "rainbow" carrots. Purple cauliflower can be found in gourmet grocery stores, but it's becoming more commonly available in regular stores as well.

Purple Salad

¼ small red cabbage
1 large purple carrot
4 oz (110 g) cooked chicken
  breast (optional)
¼ cup (25 g) dried tart cherries
2 tablespoons prepared raspberry vinaigrette

1 Remove core from the cabbage, cut into thin slices.

2 Grate the carrot on the large holes of a box grater.

3 If using, shred the chicken by pulling it apart with
two forks.

4 Add cabbage, carrot, chicken, cherries and dressing
to a medium mixing bowl. Toss until combined.

PURPLE
FOODS USED IN
THIS BENTO

Purple cabbage, Purple carrot, Dried
cherries, Purple cauliflower, Plums,
Red grapes, Beet hummus.

OTHER IDEAS FOR
PURPLE FOODS

Beets, Currants, Dragonfruit,
Eggplant, Figs, Fruit leather,
Purple pepper, Purple
potatoes, Raisins.

Brown Bento Box

Breakfast for lunch is doubly fun when it comes in the form of a sweet brown bear bagel. Load the rest of the lunch box up with other brown treats—bacon, pear and dates—for a bento your child will adore.

2 slices of cooked bacon
Pretzel bagel
Nutella
½ banana, sliced
Pear
Fruit leather
2 raisins or dried cranberries
Medjool dates

EQUIPMENT
Divided bento box (PlanetBox Shuttle)
Fruit Fresh powder
Bear face punch
Brown baking cup
Bear decorative picks

Assembly

1 Cut the bacon strips in half and spread them across the bottom of the larger compartment of the bento box.

2 Slice the bagel and spread each side with a thin layer of Nutella. Cover the bottom half of the bagel with the banana slices, positioning two of the slices partway off the edge so they look like the bear's ears. Put the top on the bagel.

3 Cut a small circle off the side of the pear. Sprinkle the cut side of the pear with Fruit Fresh powder to keep it from turning brown. Nestle the pear slice in the bagel's center hole.

4 Use the punch to cut the bear's mouth from a piece of the fruit leather. Place the mouth on the slice of pear.

5 Dab a little Nutella on the back of the raisins and stick them to the bagel for the bear's eyes. Place the bagel in the bento box.

6 Slice some of the remaining pear and put it in the baking cup in the lunch box.

7 Add dates to the remaining space in the bento and spear them with the bear picks.

BROWN FOODS USED IN THIS BENTO

Bacon, Bagel, Nutella, Pear, Raisins, Dates.

OTHER IDEAS FOR BROWN FOODS

Beef, Cereal, Chocolate Crackers, Hamburger, Lamb, Meatballs, Nuts, Pinto beans, Pretzels, Sausage, Whole wheat bread.

Black Bento Box

I admit it—pandas are black and white—but they're so cute, how could I resist adding them to this bento box? I used an onigiri set that I found online to make the rice balls in this bento. This makes it very fast and easy to make supercute pandas, but if you can't find a set like this, you can make the onigiri by hand and cut the nori with a pair of scissors to achieve a similar outcome.

Cooked sushi rice
Nori sheet
Blackberries
Black grapes

EQUIPMENT
Single-tier bento box with divider
Bear-shaped onigiri mold and panda nori
  punch (came together in a set)
Decorative waxed paper
Decorative bento picks: hats, bow and
  pandas
Panda baran (food dividers)

Assembly

1 Salt the rice and pack it firmly into the bear-shaped onigiri mold. Remove it from the mold, taking care not to disconnect the ears. Repeat twice more so you have 3 onigiri.

2 Use the punch to create three sets of face details for the onigiri. Add the ears, eyes and mouth to each of the rice balls. If you are having trouble getting the nori to stick to the rice, dip your finger in a little water and rub it into the rice to moisten it a little. Be careful not to go overboard with the water.

3 Add the hat and bow picks to the onigiri.

4 Trim the decorative waxed paper to fit in one half of the bento and add it to the box. Place the onigiri on top of it.

5 Fill half of the other side of the box with blackberries.

6 Insert the panda baran and fill the remaining quarter of the box with the grapes.

7 Poke the panda picks into the grapes and berries.

BLACK FOODS USED IN THIS BENTO
Nori, Blackberries, Black grapes.

OTHER IDEAS FOR BLACK FOODS
Black beans, Black olives, Raisins.

Sources

Amazon.com—http://www.amazon.com: Search for "bento" to find a good assortment of bento boxes and accessories. Amazon is also a great place to buy cookie cutters and decorative picks.

Bentgo—https://bentgo.com/: A single-layer divided bento box (see page 59).

Bento&co—http://en.bentoandco.com: Bento boxes, accessories and many kits that include the basic items needed to get started with bento.

BentoUSA—http://www.bentousa.com: A huge selection of bento boxes and accessories at reasonable prices.

Daiso Japan—http://www.daisojapan.com: Daiso offers inexpensive bento boxes, decorative picks, silicone and paper cups and other accessorites. Their brick-and-mortar stores offer an even larger selection of supplies.

EasyLunchboxes—http://www.easylunchboxes.com: These divided containers (see pages 25, 27, 41, 43, 79, 89 and 95) come in packs of four, which is handy if you make multiple lunches per day.

eBay.com—http://www.ebay.com: Search for "bento" to find an every changing line-up of bento boxes and accessories. Many items are shipped from overseas and are difficult to find in the states.

EcoLunchbox—https://ecolunchboxes.com/: Stainless-steel stacking bento boxes (see pages 63 and 77).

LunchBots—http://www.lunchbots.com: Single-layer stainless-steel bento boxes (see pages 71, 83, 85, 103 and 111).

OmieBox—https://www.omielife.com/: Divided bento box with an integrated thermal jar for hot or cold foods (see pages 23 and 37).

PlanetBox—http://www.planetbox.com: A single-layer divided tray (see pages 21, 33, 51, 53, 55, 87, 91 and 113).

Wilton—http://www.wilton.com: Cookie cutters, cupcake picks, icing eyes, silicone molds and other items designed for baking but handy for bento.

Yumbox—https://www.yumboxlunch.com/: A single-layer divided bento box (see pages 31, 39, 45, 47, 61, 65, 81, 101 109).

Index

Published by Tuttle Publishing, an imprint of
Periplus Editions (HK) Ltd.

www.tuttlepublishing.com

ISBN: 978-4-8053-1534-7

DISTRIBUTED BY
North America, Latin America & Europe
Tuttle Publishing
364 Innovation Drive
North Clarendon, VT 05759-9436 U.S.A.
Tel: (802) 773-8930
Fax: (802) 773-6993
info@tuttlepublishing.com
www.tuttlepublishing.com

Japan
Tuttle Publishing
Yaekari Building 3rd Floor
5-4-12 Osaki
Shinagawa-ku
Tokyo 141-0032
Tel: (81) 3 5437-0171
Fax: (81) 3 5437-0755
sales@tuttle.co.jp
www.tuttle.co.jp

Asia Pacific
Berkeley Books Pte. Ltd.
3 Kallang Sector #04-01
Singapore 349278
Tel: (65) 6741 2178
Fax: (65) 6741 2179
inquiries@periplus.com.sg
www.tuttlepublishing.com

24 23 22 21   10 9 8 7 6 5 4 3 2 1
Printed in Malaysia   2105VP

TUTTLE PUBLISHING® is a registered
trademark of Tuttle Publishing, a division of
Periplus Editions (HK) Ltd.

"Books to Span the East and West"

Tuttle Publishing was founded in 1832 in the small New England town of Rutland, Vermont [USA]. Our core values remain as strong today as they were then—to publish best-in-class books which bring people together one page at a time. In 1948, we established a publishing office in Japan—and Tuttle is now a leader in publishing English-language books about the arts, languages and cultures of Asia. The world has become a much smaller place today and Asia's economic and cultural influence has grown. Yet the need for meaningful dialogue and information about this diverse region has never been greater. Over the past seven decades, Tuttle has published thousands of books on subjects ranging from martial arts and paper crafts to language learning and literature—and our talented authors, illustrators, designers and photographers have won many prestigious awards. We welcome you to explore the wealth of information available on Asia at **www.tuttlepublishing.com**.